SADHANA
A WAY TO GOD

SADHANA
A WAY TO GOD

Christian Exercises
in Eastern Form

COMPLETE AND UNABRIDGED

by
Anthony de Mello, S.J.

An Image Book
Doubleday
NEW YORK   LONDON   TORONTO   SYDNEY   AUCKLAND

Image Books edition published September 1984
by special arrangement with Center for Spiritual Exchange

Imprimi Potest: Bertram Philipps, S.J.
                     Praep. Prov. Bomb.

Imprimatur: ✠C. Gomes, S.J.
                     Bishop of Ahmedabad
                     January 24, 1978

An Image Book
Published by Doubleday, a division of
Bantam Doubleday Dell Publishing Group, Inc.,
666 Fifth Avenue, New York, New York 10103

Image, Doubleday and the portrayal of a cross
intersecting a circle are trademarks of Doubleday, a
division of Bantam Doubleday Dell Publishing Group, Inc.

Library of Congress Cataloging in Publication Data
De Mello, Anthony, 1931–
Sadhana, a way to God.
"Complete and unabridged."
1. Spiritual exercises.   I. Title.
BX2182.2.D39   1984b   248.3   84-6735

8   10   9   7

CONTENTS

DEVOTION   105

INTRODUCTION

I have spent the past fifteen years of my life as retreat master and spiritual director helping people to pray. I hear dozens of people complain that they do not know how to pray; that, in spite of all their efforts, they seem to make no progress in prayer; that they find prayer dull and frustrating. I hear many spiritual directors confess helplessness when it comes to teaching people how to pray or, to put it more exactly, how to get satisfaction and fulfillment from prayer.

This always amazes me because I have found it relatively easy to help people to pray. I do not attribute this merely to some personal charisma I have. I attribute it to some very simple theories that I follow in my own prayer life and in guiding others in the matter of prayer. One theory is that prayer is an exercise that brings fulfillment and satisfaction and it is perfectly legitimate to seek these from prayer. Another is that prayer is to be made less with the head than with the heart. In fact, the sooner it gets away from the head and from thinking the more enjoyable and the more profitable it is likely to become. Most priests and religious equate prayer with thinking. That is their downfall.

A Jesuit friend once told me that he approached a Hindu guru for initiation in the art of prayer. The guru said to him, *"Concentrate on your breathing."* My friend proceeded to do just that for about five minutes. Then the guru said, *"The air you breathe is God. You are breathing God in and out. Become aware of that, and stay with that awareness."* My friend, after mentally making a slight theological adjustment to that statement, followed these instructions—for hours on end, day after day—and discovered, to his amazement, that prayer can be as simple a matter as breathing in and out. And he discovered in this exercise a depth and satisfaction and spiritual nourishment that he hadn't found in the many, many hours he had devoted to prayer over a period of many years.

The exercises I propose in this book are very much in line with the approach of that Hindu guru, whom I have never met or heard of since. I hold a number of theories too in the matter of prayer, but I shall speak of them in conjunction with the exercises that follow and explain how they lie behind the exercises.

I have frequently proposed these exercises to groups of people. I call them *Prayer Groups* or, more accurately, *Contemplation Groups*. Contrary to common belief, there is such a thing as group contemplation. In fact, in certain circumstances, contemplation is practiced more fruitfully in a group than alone. I have written out the exercises here almost exactly in the form and in the language in which I propose them to groups. If you plan to conduct a Contemplation Group and use this book as text, all you have to do is take the text of each exercise and read it slowly to the group and have the group follow the instructions you read to them. The reading will obviously have to be done slowly, and plenty of pauses will be needed, especially at the places that are marked: . . .

Merely reading this text to others will not make you a good leader of a Contemplation Group. For that you will have to be something of an expert in contemplation yourself. You will have to have experienced some of the things you are reading to the others. And you will have to have some skills in the art of spiritual direction. These exercises are no substitute for personal experience and spiritual expertise. But they will serve as a good beginning, and they will certainly do you and your group some good. I have taken care to exclude from this book exercises that require the guidance of a prayer specialist. And if there is any danger of harm being done through any of the exercises that follow, I shall point it out and indicate the way to avoid the harm.

I dedicate this book to the Blessed Virgin Mary, who has always been for me a model of contemplation. She has been more: I am convinced that it is her intercession that has obtained for me, and for many of the people I have guided, graces in prayer that we should never have acquired otherwise. There, then, is my first piece of advice to you if you would make progress in the art of contemplation: Seek her patronage and ask for her intercession before you start out on this way. She has been given the charisma of drawing down the Holy Spirit on the Church, as she did at the Annunciation and at Pentecost, when she prayed with the Apostles. If you get her to pray with you and for you, you will be very fortunate indeed.

AWARENESS

Exercise 1: The Riches of Silence

"Silence is the great revelation," said Lao-tse. We are accustomed to think of Scripture as the revelation of God. And so it is. I want you now to discover the revelation that silence brings. To take in the revelation that Scripture offers, you must expose yourself to Scripture. To take in the revelation that silence offers you must first attain silence. And this is not easy. Let us attempt to do this in our very first exercise.

    I want each of you to take a comfortable posture. Close your eyes.

    I am now going to invite you to keep silence for a period of ten minutes. First you will try to attain silence, as total a silence as possible of heart and mind. Having attained it, you will expose yourself to whatever revelation it brings.

    At the end of ten minutes I shall invite you to open your eyes and share with us, if you wish, what you did and what you experienced in these ten minutes.

....

....

....

    In sharing with the rest of us what you did and what happened to you, tell us what attempts you made to attain silence and how successful your attempts were. Describe this silence if you can. Tell us what you experienced in this silence. Tell us anything you thought and felt during this exercise.

The experience of people who attempt this exercise is infinitely varied. Most people discover, to their surprise, that silence is something they are simply not accustomed to. That no matter what they do they cannot still the constant wandering of their mind or quieten an emotional turmoil they feel within their heart. Others feel themselves approaching the frontiers of silence. Then they panic and withdraw. Silence can be a frightening experience.

No reason to be discouraged. Even those wandering thoughts of yours are a great revelation, aren't they? The fact that your mind wanders, isn't that a revelation about yourself? It is not enough to know this. You must take time to *experience* this wandering mind. And the *type* of wandering it indulges in—how revealing that is too!

And here's something encouraging for you: The fact that you were aware of your mental wanderings or of your inner turmoil or of your inability to be still shows that you have some small degree of silence within you, at least a sufficient amount of silence to be aware of all of this.

> Close your eyes again and become aware of your wandering mind . . . for just two minutes . . .
> Now sense the silence that makes it possible for you to be aware of the wanderings of your mind . . .

It is this minimal silence that you have within you that we shall build on in the exercises that follow. As it grows it will reveal to you more and more about yourself. Or, more accurately, silence will reveal yourself to you. That is its first revelation: your *self*. And in and through this revelation you will attain things that money cannot buy, things like wisdom and serenity and joy and God.

To attain these priceless things it is not enough for you to reflect, talk, discuss. What you will need is work. Get to work right now.

> Close your eyes. Seek silence for another five minutes.
> At the end of the exercise note whether your attempts this time are more successful or less.

Note whether silence revealed something to you this time that you failed to notice last time.

Don't seek for anything sensational in the revelation that silence brings—lights, inspirations, insights. In fact, don't *seek* at all. Limit yourself to *observing*. Just take in everything that comes to your awareness. Everything, no matter how trite and ordinary, that is thus *revealed* to you. All your revelation may consist of is the fact that your hands are clammy or that you have an urge to change your posture or that you are worried about your health. No matter. The important thing is that you have become aware of this. The content of your awareness is less important than the quality of the awareness. As the quality improves, your silence will deepen. And as your silence deepens, you will experience change. And you will discover, to your delight, that revelation is not knowledge. Revelation is power; a mysterious power that brings transformation.

Exercise 2: Body Sensations

Take up a posture that is comfortable and restful. Close your eyes.

I am now going to ask you to become aware of certain sensations in your body that you are feeling at this present moment, but of which you are not explicitly aware . . . Be aware of the touch of your clothes on your shoulders . . . Now become aware of the touch of your clothes on your back, or of your back touching the back of the chair you are sitting on . . . Now be aware of the feel of your hands as they touch each other or rest on your lap . . . Now become conscious of your thighs or your buttocks pressing against your chair . . . Now the feel of your feet touching your shoes . . . Now become explicitly aware of your sitting posture . . .

Once again: your shoulders . . . your back . . . your right

hand . . . your left hand . . . your thighs . . . your feet
. . . your sitting posture . . .

Again: shoulders . . . back . . . right hand . . . left hand
. . . right thigh . . . left thigh . . . right foot . . . left foot
. . . sitting posture . . .

Continue to go the round by yourself now, moving from one
part of your body to the other. Do not dwell for more than a
couple of seconds on each part, shoulders, back, thighs, etc.
. . . Keep moving from one to the other . . .

You may dwell either on the parts of the body I have indicated or on any other parts you wish: your head, your neck,
your arms, your chest, your stomach . . . The important
thing is that you get the *feel*, the sensation of each part, that you
feel it for a second or two and then move on to another part of
the body . . .

After five minutes I shall ask you to open your eyes gently
and end the exercise.

This simple exercise brings an immediate sense of relaxedness
to most people. In most groups, when I first propose this exercise, someone or other becomes so relaxed that he drops off to
sleep!

One of the biggest enemies to prayer is nervous tension. This
exercise helps you to deal with that. The formula is a simple one:
You relax when you come to your senses; when you become as
fully conscious as possible of your body sensations, of the sounds
around you, of your breathing, of the taste of something in your
mouth.

Far too many people live too much *in their head*—they are
mostly conscious of the thinking and fantasizing that is going on
in their head and far too little conscious of the activity of their
senses. As a result they rarely live in the present. They are almost
always in the past or in the future. In the past, regretting past
mistakes, feeling guilty about past sins, gloating over past
achievements, resenting past injuries caused them by other peo-

ple. Or in the future, dreading possible calamities and unpleas-
antnesses, anticipating future joys, dreaming of future events.

Recalling the past in order to profit from it, or even to enjoy it
afresh, and anticipating the future in order to plan realistically
are valuable functions, provided they do not take us out of the
present for too long. To succeed in prayer it is essential to develop the ability to make contact with the present and to stay
there. And there is no better method I know of for staying in the
present than getting out of your head and returning to your
senses.

Feel the heat or cold of the atmosphere around you. Feel the
breeze as it caresses your body. Feel the heat of the sun making
contact with your skin. Feel the texture and temperature of the
object you are touching . . . and see what a difference it makes.
See how you come alive by coming to the present. Once you have
mastered this technique of sense awareness you will be surprised
to see what it does to you if you are the type that frequently
worries about the future or feels guilty about the past.

A word about getting out of your head: The head is not a very
good place for prayer. It is not a bad place for *starting* your
prayer. But if your prayer stays there too long and doesn't move
into the heart, it will gradually dry up and prove tiresome and
frustrating. You must learn to move out of the area of thinking
and talking and move into the area of feeling, sensing, loving,
intuiting. That is the area where contemplation is born and
prayer becomes a transforming power and a source of never-
ending delight and peace.

It is just possible that some people—a very few—will feel, as a
result of this exercise, not relaxedness and peace but an increase
of tension. If this happens to you switch to the awareness of your
tension. Note what part of your body is tense. Note exactly what
the tension feels like. Become aware of the fact that you are
tensing yourself and note exactly how you are doing this.

When I use the word *note* I refer not to reflection but to feeling
and sensing. I cannot repeat too often that this exercise is a

matter of feeling, not thinking. There actually are people who, when asked to feel their arms or legs or hands, do not really *feel* them. They produce a mental picture of these limbs of theirs. They *know* where these limbs are situated and they become aware of this knowledge. But they do not *feel* the limbs themselves. Where other people feel a leg or hand, all these people feel is a blank. All they have is a mental picture.

The best way to overcome this defect (and to make sure that you are not taking a mental picture for a felt experience) is to pick up as many sensations as you can in each of these limbs: your shoulders, your back, your thighs, your hands, your feet. This will also help you to sympathize with people who do not feel their limbs because you will very probably discover that only a small part of the surface of these limbs yields sensations at the start. You may pick up no sensations at all over large areas of your body. That is because your sensibility has been deadened from so much living in your head. The surface of your skin is covered with trillions of biochemical reactions that we call sensations and here you are finding it hard to pick up even a few of them! You have hardened yourself not to feel—very likely because of some emotional hurt or conflict that you have long since forgotten. And your perception, your awareness, your powers of concentration and attention are still gross and underdeveloped.

At a later stage I shall explain what relation this exercise has to prayer and how, for many people, the exercise itself is a form of contemplation. For the time being let it suffice as a preparation for prayer and contemplation, as a means for attaining relaxation and stillness, without which prayer becomes difficult, even impossible.

Close your eyes once again. Get in touch with sensations in various parts of your body.

The ideal would be to not even think of the various parts of your body as "hands" or "legs" or "back" but just to move from one sensation to another and give no labels or names to your limbs and organs as you sense them.

If you notice an urge to move or to shift your position, do not give in to it. Just become aware of the urge and the bodily discomfort, if any, that gives rise to the urge.

Stay with this exercise for a few minutes. You will gradually feel a certain stillness in your body. Do not explicitly rest in the stillness. Go on with your awareness exercise and leave the stillness to take care of itself.

If you become distracted, get back to the awareness of body sensations, moving from one to another, until your body becomes still once again and your mind quietens with your body and you are able to sense once again this stillness that brings peace and a foretaste of contemplation and of God. However, I repeat, do not explicitly rest in the stillness.

Why not rest in the stillness that you will probably experience during this exercise? Resting in it can be relaxing and even delightful. But if you do so, you run the danger of inducing a mild trance or a mental blank and resting in this trance, which leads you nowhere as far as contemplation is concerned. It is a little like self-hypnosis that has nothing to do either with the sharpening of awareness or with contemplation.

So it is important that you not deliberately seek to produce any stillness or silence within you and not explicitly rest in it when it occurs. What you must seek is a sharpening of awareness rather than the deadening of awareness that comes from a trance, however mild. So, in spite of the stillness, and within the stillness, you must keep to your exercise of awareness and leave the stillness to take care of itself.

There will be moments when the stillness or the *blank* will be so powerful that it will make all exercise and all effort on your part impossible. In such moments it is no longer you who go in quest of stillness. It is stillness that takes possession of you and overwhelms you. When this happens, you may safely, and profitably, let go of all effort (which has become impossible, anyway) and surrender to this overpowering stillness within you.

Exercise 3:   Body Sensations. Thought Control

This exercise is a deepening of the previous one. The previous exercise may have seemed a very simple one to you—so simple, in fact, as to prove disillusioning. But contemplation is a very simple thing, really. To advance in it what you need is not to complicate your techniques but to persevere in simplicity, a thing that most people find very, very hard. Put up with your boredom. Resist the temptation to seek novelty and, instead, seek depth.

To get the full benefit of this and the previous exercise, you will have to practice them over a long period of time. I once made a Buddhist retreat at which we spent as many as twelve to fourteen hours each day concentrating on our breathing, on the air coming in and going out of our nostrils. No variety, no excitement, no thought content with which to keep our minds entertained! I vividly remember the day we dedicated some twelve hours and more to becoming aware of all the sensations in the tiny area between the nostrils and the upper lip! Most of us drew a blank for hours on end and it was only by dint of patient, persevering effort at concentration and awareness that this stubborn area began to yield its sensations.

What is the benefit of all this from the point of view of prayer, you will ask. The only reply I shall give you for now is: Don't ask questions. Do what you are asked to and you will discover the answer for yourself. Truth is found less in words and explanations than in action and experience. So get to work, with faith and perseverance (and you are going to need a good supply of these!) and before long you will *experience* the answer to your questions.

You will also experience a disinclination to answer the questions, even seemingly practical questions, of others on these matters. What all those questions are really saying is, *"Show me."* And the only worthy answer to them is, *"Open your eyes and see for yourself."* I'd rather you walked with me to the top of the mountain and experienced the sunrise than have myself embark upon glowing accounts of what the sunrise does to you when you gaze at it from the top of the mountain. *"Come and see,"* said Jesus to two of his questioning disciples. Very wise!

All the glory of a mountain sunrise, and much, much more, is contained in so drab an exercise as being aware of your body sensations for hours and days on end. Come and see for yourself! You will not, in all likelihood, have the leisure to give it whole hours and days. I suggest that you begin each period of prayer with this exercise. Keep to it till you find peace and stillness and then move on to your prayer, whatever be the type and form of prayer you generally practice. You can do this very profitably at other times of the day too, at odd moments when you are waiting for a bus or train, when you are tired and strained and want a little relaxation, when you have a few minutes to waste and don't know what to do with them.

The time will come, hopefully, when you will experience a great relish and delight in this awareness and you will not want to move on to any other form of prayer. That may be the time for you to just stay with it and discover the deep and genuine contemplation hidden within the depths of this humble exercise. Of this kind of contemplation I shall speak later.

Let us move on to our next exercise now. It is easily described in a few sentences. But it needs to be repeated and practiced frequently. In my contemplation groups I never fail to begin with at least a few minutes of these exercises each time we come together, and I recommend the group members to practice them daily for at least a few minutes morning, noon, and night.

Close your eyes. Repeat the previous exercise, moving from one part of your body to another and becoming aware of all the sensations you can pick up in each part. Do this for from five to ten minutes.

Now choose just one small area of your face: your forehead, for instance, or a cheek or your chin. Try to pick up every sensation you can in this area.

At the beginning the area may seem completely devoid of sensation. If this happens then revert to the previous exercise for a while. Then come back to this area. And keep doing this till you notice some sensation there, no matter how faint. Once you notice some sensation, stay with it. It may disappear. It may change into another sensation. Other sensations may sprout up around it.

Be aware of the type of sensations that emerge: itching, pricking, burning, pulling, vibrating, throbbing, numbness . . .

If your mind wanders, bring it patiently back to the exercise as soon as you become aware of the wandering.

I shall end this chapter by suggesting a sister exercise for use outside the time of prayer. When you walk, become aware, for a while, of the motion of your legs. You can do this anywhere, even on a crowded street. It is not a question of knowing that your legs are moving but of getting the *feel* of the movement. This will have a soothing, tranquilizing effect on you. You might even make a concentration exercise out of this, but then you must do this in a quiet place where you are not likely to be seen by others who may, quite understandably, conclude from watching you that there is something seriously the matter with you! Here is the exercise:

While pacing up and down a room or corridor slow down your movement to the extent that you are fully aware of each of the movements of your legs. Become aware of the following: the lifting of your left foot . . . the movement forward of the left foot . . . the left foot touching the ground . . . the weight of your body shifting onto your left leg . . .

Now the lifting of your right foot . . . its movement forward . . . its coming to rest on the ground in front of you . . . and so on.

As an aid to concentration you might say to yourself mentally as you lift your foot, *"Lifting . . . lifting . . . lifting . . ."* As you move it forward, *"Moving . . . moving . . . moving . . ."* And as you place it down on terra firma, ". . . *placing . . . placing."*

This exercise is most emphatically *not* recommended for moments when you are in a hurry! And you have only to do it once to understand why I would dissuade you from doing it in any place where you are likely to be seen by any but the most nonjudgmental of men!

Exercise 4: Thought Control

Most people have trouble with distractions during their awareness exercises, so I want to say something here about how to deal with these distractions.

You may find it a help in dealing with distractions to keep your eyes not closed but slightly open. Open enough for you to be able to see some three feet ahead of you. Then let your eyes rest on one spot or on an object. Do not focus on that spot or object, however, or concentrate on it or make it the object of your explicit attention.

Some people have difficulty being concentrated when their eyes are closed. It is as if those closed eyes form a blank screen upon which their mind can project all sorts of thoughts that draw them away from their concentration. Hence the suggestion to keep your eyes half open, resting on an object or a spot some three feet away. Experiment with this but take the advice only if it helps you. You may be one of those people who find that half-open eyes leave you as exposed to distractions as do closed eyes.

Another help in dealing with distractions is, believe it or not, having your back erect. I have as yet discovered no scientific reason for this. But I am convinced from my own and others'

experience that this is so. The ideal posture for this is the lotus
posture that students of yoga are taught: legs intertwined with
feet resting upon opposite thighs and spine erect. I am told that
people who manage to attain this posture have such little difficulty with distractions that they actually have trouble thinking
and getting their thinking mind to function at all. Hence this
posture is said to be ideally suited for contemplation and concentration.

Most of you will not have the patience and the courage to
master this extremely difficult, though rewarding, posture. You
will have to content yourself with either sitting upright against a
straight-backed chair or sitting on the edge of a chair to keep your
back straight. This is not quite as uncomfortable as appears at
first sight. On the contrary, you will find as time goes by that a
curved spine is far more uncomfortable. And you will probably
discover that the straight back does your concentration a world of
good. I have it on good authority that some Zen masters are able
to walk into a meditation hall and tell, merely from the position of
a meditator's back, whether he is distracted or not. This seems a
somewhat exaggerated claim to me because I can certainly recall
times when, coming out of meditation, my back was far from
erect, yet I hadn't been distracted.

Some advocates of the straight back go so far as to advise lying
flat on your back on a hard surface like the floor if there is no
other way you can comfortably keep your back straight. A valuable suggestion, as far as it goes, and one worth experimenting
with. My only reservation against it is that lying on one's back
generally sends most people off to sleep, a state of mind that is
generally even more disastrous to contemplation than are distractions.

It is quite likely that for all your attempts to deal with your
distractions through the proper positioning of your eyes and
back you are still plagued with a wandering mind. No cause for
alarm. A wandering mind is an occupational nuisance that every
serious contemplative has to grapple with. The struggle for con-

trol of the mind is long and arduous but very well worth attempting for the great fruit it eventually brings. So there is no substitute, really, for much patience and perseverance—and faith that you will eventually succeed in spite of much discouraging evidence to the contrary.

I have one more suggestion to offer you as a help here. It is the most effective way I have as yet discovered for dealing with distractions. I shall put it in the form of an exercise.

Close your eyes, or leave them half open if you find that more helpful.

Now observe every thought that comes into your mind. There are two ways of dealing with thoughts. One is to follow them around as a puppy in the streets will follow any pair of legs it finds in motion, no matter in what direction they are moving. The other is to observe them as a man stationed at his window watches passers-by on the street. This is the way I want you to observe your thoughts.

After you have done this for a while, become aware that you are thinking. You may even say to yourself interiorly, *I am thinking . . . I am thinking . . .* or more briefly, *Thinking . . . thinking . . .* to keep yourself aware of the thinking process that is going on within you.

If you find there are no thoughts in your mind and your mind is blank, wait for the next thought to make its appearance. Be on the alert and, as soon as the thought appears, become aware of it or of the fact that you are thinking.

Keep up this exercise for three or four minutes.

During this exercise you may make the surprising discovery that while you are aware of the fact that you are thinking all thinking tends to stop!

Here, then, is a simple way of dealing with a wandering mind. Pause for a while and turn to the fact that you are thinking and the thinking will cease temporarily. Keep this exercise for times when you are more than ordinarily distracted. It is almost impossible not to be frequently distracted when you first launch out into the field of contemplation. But most distractions are dealt with by simply recalling the mind to its task of concentration when you are aware of the distraction. There is no need for this exercise except when your mind is more than ordinarily distracted.

There is a type of distraction that is charged with strong emotion: love, fear, resentment, or some other emotion. This kind of distraction with a strong emotional base will not easily yield to the exercise I have just suggested. Other methods that I shall suggest later will have to be called into service; and, above all, you will have to have acquired considerable skill in the art of concentration and contemplation to maintain your peace in the face of this kind of distraction.

Exercise 5:   Breathing Sensations

Begin this exercise by spending some five minutes in becoming aware of sensations in various parts of your body . . . .

Now move on to the awareness of your breathing. Become aware of the air as it comes in and goes out through your nostrils . . .

Do not concentrate on the air as it enters your lungs. Limit your awareness to the air as it passes through your nostrils . . .

Do not control your breathing. Do not attempt to deepen it. This is not an exercise in breathing but in awareness. So if your breathing is shallow, leave it that way. Do not interfere with it. Observe it.

Each time you are distracted, return with vigor to your task. In fact, before you get started it will help if you resolve firmly not to miss awareness of a single breath.

Continue this exercise for some ten or fifteen minutes.

Most people find this exercise more difficult to do than the previous two exercises. And yet, from the point of view of sharpening awareness, it is the most rewarding of the three. It also has the effect of bringing calmness and relaxation with it.

In attempting to be aware of your breathing, do not tense your muscles. Determination must not be confounded with nervous tension. You must expect to be considerably distracted at the beginning. No matter how distracted you are, the mere fact that you keep returning again and again to the awareness of your breathing—the mere effort involved in doing this—will bring beneficial effects that you will gradually notice.

Once you have developed some proficiency in this exercise, move on to a somewhat more difficult and more effective variant:

Become aware of the sensation of the air passing through your nostrils. Feel its touch. Notice in what part of the nostrils you feel the touch of the air when you inhale . . . and in what part of the nostrils you feel the touch of the air when you exhale . . .

Become aware, if you can, of the warmth or coldness of the air . . . its coldness when it comes in, its warmth when it goes out.

You may also be aware that the quantity of air that passes through one nostril is greater than the amount that passes through the other . . .

Be sensitive and alert to the slightest, lightest touch of the air on your nostrils as you inhale and exhale . . .

Stay with this awareness for some ten or fifteen minutes.

The time indicated for each of these exercises is the minimum amount of time required for you to get some idea of the value of the exercise and for you to benefit from it. But the more time you are able to give to the exercise the greater, obviously, will be the fruit you will derive from it.

The only qualification I would make to that statement is this: Do not stay on the awareness of breathing alone for many hours at a stretch over a period of more than two or three days. It may happen that this exercise brings you great peace and a sense of depth and fullness that delights you and you might venture into many hours of this during a retreat when you are in silence for a number of days. Do not do this unless you have a competent guide available. The reason is that prolonged concentration on so subtle a function as breathing is likely to produce hallucinations or to draw out material from the unconscious that you may not be able to control. The danger is remote, true, and the likelihood that someone will go in for this sort of exercise for hours at a stretch is a very slim one. But I'd much rather you were aware of it all the same.

I cannot sufficiently extol the value of this exercise for people who desire to attain peace and self-control and a deep inner joy in the midst of troubles. One famous oriental master would say to his disciples, *"Your breathing is your greatest friend. Return to it in all your troubles and you will find comfort and guidance."* A mysterious statement—and one that you will be inclined to agree with after you have invested a sufficient amount of time in mastering the difficult art of awareness.

AWARENESS AND CONTEMPLATION

This, perhaps, is the time to deal with the objection, sometimes raised in my Contemplation Groups, that these awareness exercises, while they may help for relaxation, have nothing to do with contemplation in the way we Christians understand the word, and most certainly are not prayer.

I shall now attempt to explain how these simple exercises can be taken to be contemplation in the strict Christian sense of the word. If the explanation does not satisfy you or only creates problems for you, then I suggest that you put aside all I say about this matter and practice these awareness exercises merely as a means for disposing yourself for prayer and contemplation, or just ignore these exercises altogether and move on to others in this book that are more to your taste.

Let me first explain my use of the words prayer and contemplation. I use the word prayer to mean communication with God that is carried on mainly through the use of words and images and thoughts. I shall propose many exercises, later on, that I consider to come under the heading of prayer. Contemplation for me is communication with God that makes a minimal use of words, images, and concepts or dispenses with words, images, and concepts altogether. This is the sort of prayer that John of the Cross speaks of in his *Dark Night of the Soul* or the author of *The Cloud of Unknowing* explains in his admirable book. Some of the exercises that I propose in this book connected with the Jesus Prayer could be considered to be either prayer or contemplation or a blending of both, depending on how much emphasis you place on words and thoughts in your use of the exercises.

And now to the heart of our problem: When I practice the exercise of being aware of my body sensations or of my breathing, can I be said to be communicating with God? The answer is Yes. Let me explain the nature of this *communicating with God* that takes place in the awareness exercises.

Many mystics tell us that, in addition to the mind and heart with which we ordinarily communicate with God, we are, all of us, endowed with a mystical mind and mystical heart, a faculty which makes it possible for us to know God directly, to grasp and *intuit* him in his very being, though in a dark manner, apart from all thoughts and concepts and images.

Ordinarily all our contact with God is indirect—through images and concepts that necessarily distort his reality. To be able to grasp him beyond these thoughts and images is the privilege of this faculty which, in the course of this explanation, I shall call the Heart (a word dear to the author of *The Cloud of Unknowing*, though it has nothing to do with our physical heart or our affectivity).

In most of us this Heart lies dormant and undeveloped. If it were to be awakened it would be constantly straining toward God and, given a chance, would impel the whole of our being toward him. But for this, it needs to be developed, it needs to have the dross that surrounds it removed so that it can be attracted toward the Eternal Magnet.

The dross is the vast number of thoughts and words and images that we constantly interpose between ourselves and God when we are communicating with him. Words sometimes serve to impede rather than foster communication and intimacy. Silence —of words and thoughts—can sometimes be the most powerful form of communication and union when hearts are full of love. Our communication with God, however, is not quite so simple a matter. I can gaze lovingly into the eyes of an intimate friend and communicate with him beyond words. But what do I gaze into when I gaze silently at God? An imageless, formless reality. A blank!

Now that is just what is demanded of some people if they would go deep into communion with the Infinite, with God: gaze for hours at a blank. Some mystics recommend that we gaze at this blank *lovingly*. And it requires a good deal of faith to gaze with love and yearning at what seems like just nothing when we first get in touch with it.

Ordinarily you will never even get anywhere near this blank, even supposing an intense desire on your part to spend hours on end gazing at it, if your mind isn't silenced. As long as your mind machine keeps spinning out millions of thoughts and words, your *mystical mind* or Heart will remain underdeveloped. Notice how sharp is the hearing and the sense of touch of a blind man. He has lost his faculty of seeing and this has forced him to develop his other faculties of perception. Something similar happens in the mystical world. If we could go mentally blind, so to speak, if we could put a bandage over our mind while we are communicating with God, we would be forced to develop some other faculty for communicating with him—that faculty which, according to a

number of mystics, is already straining to move out to him anyway if it were given a chance to develop: the Heart.

When our Heart gets its first direct, dark glimpse of God it feels
like a glimpse into emptiness and blankness. People who get to
this stage frequently complain that they are doing nothing at
prayer, that they are wasting their time, that they are idle, that
nothing seems to happen, that they are in total darkness. To
escape from this uncomfortable state they, unfortunately, have
recourse once again to their thinking faculty; they take the bandage off their minds and begin to *think* and to *speak* with God—
just the one thing they need *not* do.

If God is gracious to them, and he very frequently is, he will
make it impossible for them to use their mind in prayer. They will
find all thinking distasteful; vocal prayer will be unbearable to
them because the words seem meaningless; they will just go *dry*
every time they attempt to communicate with God in any way
except the way of silence. And initially even this silence is painful
and dry. They might then slip into the biggest evil of all: they may
abandon prayer altogether because they find themselves forced,
in prayer, to choose between the frustration of not being able to
use their minds and the hollow feeling of wasting their time and
doing nothing in the darkness that meets them when they silence
their minds.

If they avoid this evil and persevere in the exercise of prayer
and expose themselves, in blind faith, to the emptiness, the darkness, the idleness, the nothingness, they will gradually discover,
at first in small flashes, later in a more permanent fashion, that
there is a glow in the darkness, that the emptiness mysteriously
fills their heart, that the idleness is full of God's activity, that in
the nothingness their being is recreated and shaped anew . . .
and all of this in a way they just cannot describe either to themselves or to others. They will just know after each such session of
prayer or contemplation, call it what you will, that something
mysterious has been working within them, bringing refreshment
and nourishment and well-being with it. They will notice they

have a yearning hunger to return to this dark contemplation that seems to make no sense and yet fills them with life, even with a mild intoxication that they can hardly perceive with their mind, they can hardly feel with their emotions, and yet is unmistakably there and so real and satisfying that they wouldn't exchange it for all the intoxication that comes from the delights that the world of the senses and the emotions and the mind has to offer. Funny that at the beginning it should have seemed so dry and dark and tasteless!

If you would attain to this state and draw close to this mystical darkness and begin to communicate with God through this Heart that the mystics speak of, the first thing you may have to do is find some means for silencing the mind. There are some fortunate people (and it is very important that you know this lest you fall into the error of thinking that everyone who would make progress in contemplation must, of necessity, pass through this process of confronting the darkness) who attain to this spontaneously without ever having to silence their discursive mind and quieten all their words and thoughts. They are like people who have all the sharpness of the blind man in their hands and ears and yet continue to enjoy the full use of their sight. They relish vocal prayer, they profit immensely from the use of their imagination in prayer, they give full rein to their thought processes while they deal with God, and beneath all this activity their Heart develops and directly intuits the Divine.

If you are not among these fortunate people you will have to do something to develop this Heart of yours. There is nothing you can do directly. All you can do is silence your discursive mind: abstain from all thoughts and words while you are at prayer and leave the Heart to develop by itself.

To silence the mind is an extremely difficult task. How hard it is to keep the mind from thinking, thinking, thinking, forever thinking, forever producing thoughts in a never-ending stream. Our Hindu masters in India have a saying: one thorn is removed by another. By this they mean that you will be wise to use one thought to rid yourself of all the other thoughts that crowd into your mind. One thought, one image, one phrase or sentence or word that your mind can be made to fasten on. For to consciously attempt to keep the mind in a *thought*less state, in a void, is to attempt the impossible. The mind must have something to occupy it. Well, then, give it something with which to occupy itself—but just one thing. An image of the Saviour that you gaze on lovingly and to which you return each time you are distracted; an ejaculation that you keep repeating ceaselessly to prevent the mind from wandering. A time will come, hopefully, when the image will disappear from consciousness, when the word will be taken out of your mouth and your discursive mind will be perfectly stilled and your Heart will be given free scope to gaze, unimpeded, into the Darkness!

As a matter of fact, you do not even have to get to this stage where the image disappears and the words are stilled to have your Heart function. The fact that your discursive mind has had its activity reduced so drastically is already an immense help for the Heart to develop and to function. So even if you never get to the imageless and the wordless state you will, quite likely, be growing in contemplation.

You will notice that the two means I have suggested, the image of the Saviour and the repetition of an ejaculation, are both overtly *religious* in nature. Keep in mind, however, that our primary purpose in this exercise is *not* the type of activity that the discursive mind engages in, but the opening up and developing of the Heart. Provided this is achieved, does it really matter whether the *thorn* you use to remove all the other thorns is a religious thorn or not? If your main purpose is to get light into your darkness, does it really matter that the candle that sheds light into your darkness is a holy candle or not? Does it matter, then, whether you concentrate on an image of the Saviour or a book or a leaf or a spot on the floor? A Jesuit friend who loves to dabble in such things (and, I suspect, test all religious theories with a healthy measure of skepticism) assures me that, through constantly saying to himself "one-two-three-four" rhythmically, he achieves the same *mystical* results that his more *religious* confreres claim to achieve through the devout and rhythmical recitation of some ejaculation! And I believe him. There is, undoubtedly, a sacramental value in the use of the *religious* thorn. But as far as our main purpose is concerned, one thorn is just as good as another.

And so we are led to the seemingly disconcerting conclusion that concentration on your breathing or your body sensations is very good contemplation in the strict sense of the word. I have had this theory of mine confirmed by some Jesuits who made a thirty-day retreat under my guidance and who agreed to give, in addition to the five hours that they were supposed to give to what we call the Ignatian exercises, four or five hours a day to this simple exercise of awareness of their breathing and of their body sensations. I was not surprised when they told me that during their awareness exercises (once they had developed some familiarity with them) their experiences were identical with the experiences they had while practicing what is known in Catholic terminology as the prayer of faith, or the prayer of quiet. Most of them even assured me that these awareness exercises led to a deepening of the prayer experiences they had formerly had, giving these experiences more vigor and sharpness, in a manner of speaking.

Later in this book, in fact right from the very next exercise, I shall be proposing exercises that are more overtly religious in tone and will satisfy the misgivings of those of you who feel uncomfortable spending a good deal of their prayer time in just awareness exercises. These overtly religious exercises will, at the same time, offer all the fruits that can be attained through the awareness exercises. They do contain a very slight measure of reflection that the awareness exercises do not have; however, the measure is so slight as to be almost negligible, so do not hesitate to choose them over the awareness exercises if that way you feel more comfortable.

I deliberately used the words "a good deal of your prayer time" in the previous paragraph. I would not have you abandon all your *prayer* (communication with God that involves the use of words, images, and concepts) in favor of *pure contemplation.* There is a time for meditation and prayer and there is a time for contemplation, just as there is a time for action and a time for contemplation. While you are engaged in what I have called *contemplation,* however, make sure you do not give in to the temptation to think —no matter how holy the thought may be. Just as in your time of prayer you would reject *holy* thoughts that are connected with your work and which are very good at their own proper time but are now a distraction to your prayer, so in your time of contemplation you must vigorously reject all thoughts of whatever nature as being destructive of this particular form of communication with God. Now is the time to expose yourself to the divine sun in silence, not to reflect on the virtues and properties of the sun's rays; now is the time to gaze lovingly into the eyes of your divine lover and not break this special intimacy with words and reflections about him. Communication through words must be put off for another occasion. Now is the time for wordless communion.

There is one important point on which I cannot, unfortunately, give you guidance in this book. For this you will need the guidance of an experienced master who is familiar with your spiritual needs. The point is: how much of the time that you set aside daily for communion with God should you give to prayer and how much to contemplation. This is something you can best decide with your spiritual director. With his help you will also have to decide whether you should go in for this kind of *contemplation* at all. Perhaps you are one of those fortunate people I spoke of earlier who have the fullest use of their hands and ears without ever having to bandage their eyes; whose mystical Heart is in the deepest possible communion with God while their mind communicates with him through words and thoughts; who do not need to keep silence to achieve, with their Beloved, the kind of intimacy that many others achieve only through silence.

If you are not able to find a spiritual director, ask God to guide you and begin by giving a few minutes each day to *contemplation* either in the form of these awareness exercises or in the form of some of the simpler exercises that follow. Even in your *prayer* time try gently to reduce the amount of thinking that you do and pray more with the heart. Saint Teresa of Ávila used to say, *"The important thing is not to think much but to love much."* So do a lot of loving during your time of prayer. And God will guide you even though it be through a period of trial and error.

Exercise 6:   God in My Breath

In the last chapter I told you I would offer you some exercises that are more explicitly religious in tone and yet contain many of the benefits of the awareness exercises. Here is one:

Close your eyes and practice the awareness of body sensations for a while . . .

Then come to the awareness of your breathing as described in the previous exercise and stay with this awareness for a few minutes . . .

I want you to reflect now that this air that you are breathing in is charged with the power and the presence of God . . . Think of the air as of an immense ocean that surrounds you . . . an ocean heavily colored with God's presence and God's being . . . While you draw the air into your lungs you are drawing God in . . .

Be aware that you are drawing in the power and presence of God each time you breathe in . . . Stay in this awareness as long as you can . . .

Notice what you feel when you become conscious that you are drawing God in with each breath you take . . .

There is a variation to this exercise. Another reflection, this one borrowed from the mentality of the Hebrews as we find them in the Bible. For them a man's breath was his life. When a man died God took his breath away; that is what made him die. If a man lived, it was because God kept putting his breath, his "spirit," into this man. It was the presence of this Spirit of God that kept the man alive.

While you breathe in, be conscious of God's Spirit coming into you . . . Fill your lungs with the divine energy he brings with him . . .

While you breathe out, imagine you are breathing out all your impurities . . . your fears . . . your negative feelings . . .

Imagine you see your whole body becoming radiant and alive through this process of breathing in God's life-giving Spirit and breathing out all your impurities . . .

Stay with this awareness as long as you can without distractions . . .

Exercise 7: Breath Communication with God

Earlier I made a distinction between prayer and contemplation. There is another way of expressing that distinction—by speaking of two types of prayer, the devotional and the intuitional.

Intuitional prayer would coincide roughly with what I called contemplation, devotional prayer with what I called prayer. Both forms of prayer lead to union with God. Each of them is more suited to some people than to others. Or the same people will find one form of prayer more suitable to their needs at one time rather than at another.

Devotional prayer too is geared to the heart, for any prayer that limits itself to the thinking mind alone is not prayer really but, at best, a preparation for prayer. Even among men there is no genuine personal communication that isn't at least in some small degree heart communication, that does not contain some small degree of emotion in it. If a communication, a sharing of *thoughts*, is entirely and totally devoid of all emotion, you can be sure the intimate, personal dimension is lacking. There is no communion leading to intimacy.

I want to give you now a variation of the previous exercise that will make the exercise more devotional than intuitional. You will notice, however, that the amount of thought content in the prayer is minimal, and so the exercise will easily move from the devotional to the intuitional, from the heart to the Heart. It will become, in fact, a good combination of the devotional and the intuitional.

Become aware of your breathing for a while . . .

Now reflect on the presence of God in the atmosphere all around you . . . Reflect on his presence in the air you are breathing . . . Be conscious of his presence in the air as you breathe in and out . . . Notice what you feel when you become conscious of his presence in the air you are breathing in and out . . .

I want you now to express yourself to God. But I want you to do this nonverbally. Frequently, expressing a sentiment through a look or a gesture makes the expression much more powerful than expressing it through words. I want you to express various sentiments to God not through words but through your breathing.

Express, first of all, a great yearning for him. Without using any words, even mentally, say to him, *"My God, I long for you . . ."* just by the way you breathe. Perhaps you will express this by breathing in deeply, by deepening your inhalation . . .

Now express another attitude or sentiment: one of trust and surrender. Without any words, just through the way you breathe, say to him, *"My God, I surrender myself entirely to you . . ."* You may want to do this by emphasizing your exhalation, by breathing out each time as if you were sighing deeply. Each

time you breathe out, feel yourself letting the whole of yourself
go in God's hands . . .

Now take up other attitudes before God and express these
through your breathing. Love . . . Closeness and Intimacy
. . . Adoration . . . Gratitude . . . Praise . . .

If you tire of doing this, return to the beginning of this
exercise and just rest peacefully in the awareness of God all
around you and in the air you are breathing in and out . . .
Then, if you tend to get distracted, fall back on the second part
of the exercise and express yourself to God nonverbally once
more . . .

Exercise 8: Stillness

This is an exercise in stillness. The Lord says, *"Be still and know
that I am God."* Modern man is unfortunately plagued by a nervous
tension that makes it almost impossible for him to be quiet. If he
wants to learn to pray he must first learn to be still, to quieten
himself. In fact, this very quietness and stillness frequently becomes prayer when God manifests himself in the form of stillness.

Repeat the exercise of becoming aware of the sensations in
your body. Only this time I want you to go over the whole of
your body, starting with the top of your head and ending with
the tips of your toes and omitting no part of the body . . .

Be aware of every sensation in each part . . . You may find
some parts of your body completely devoid of sensation . . .
Dwell on these for a few seconds—if no sensation emerges,
move on . . .

As you become more proficient in this exercise you will,
hopefully, sharpen your awareness to the extent that there will
be no part of your body in which you do not feel many sensations . . . For the time being you must be content to dwell

briefly on the *blanks* and move on to the parts where you feel
more sensations . . . Move slowly from head to foot . . .
then once again, from head to foot . . . and so on for some
fifteen minutes.

As your awareness sharpens you will pick up sensations that
you hadn't noticed before . . . you will also pick up sensations that are extremely subtle, too subtle to be perceived by
any but a man of deep concentration and deep peace.

Now become aware of your body as a whole. Feel the whole
of your body as one mass of various types of sensations . . .
Stay with this for a while, then return to the awareness by parts,
moving from head to foot . . . then, once again, rest in the
awareness of your body as a whole . . .

Notice now the deep stillness that has come over you. Notice
the complete stillness of your body . . . Do not, however, rest
in the stillness to the extent of losing awareness of your
body . . .

If you are getting distracted, give yourself the occupation of
moving once again from head to foot, becoming aware of sensations in each part of your body . . . Then, once again, notice the stillness in your body . . . If you are practicing this
exercise in a group, notice the stillness in the whole room . . .

It is very important that you do not move any part of your
body while you are doing this exercise. This will be difficult at
first, but each time you feel the urge to move, or scratch, or
fidget, become aware of this urge . . . Don't give in to it, just
become aware of it as sharply as you can . . . It will gradually
go away and you will become still once more . . .

It is extremely painful for most people to stay still. Even physically painful. They become physically tense. If you become tense,
spend all the time you need becoming aware of the tension . . .
where you feel it, what it feels like . . . and stay with it till the
tension disappears.

You may feel physical pain. No matter how comfortable the

position you have adopted for this exercise, your body is likely to protest against the stillness by developing aches and pains in various parts. When this happens, resist the temptation to move your limbs or readjust your posture so as to ease the pain. Just become keenly aware of the pain.

During a Buddhist retreat I made, we were asked to sit for a whole hour at a stretch without moving. I happened to be sitting cross-legged and the pain in my knees and back became so intense it was excruciating. I do not remember ever having suffered so much physical pain in all my life. We were supposed, during that hour, to be aware of our body sensations, moving from one part of the body to another. My awareness was wholly absorbed by the acute pain in my knees. I was sweating profusely. And I thought I should faint with the pain—until I decided not to fight it, not to run away from it, not to desire to alleviate it, but to become aware of it, to identify with it. I broke the pain sensation up into its component parts and I discovered, to my surprise, that it was composed of many sensations, not just one: there was an intense burning sensation, a pulling and tugging, a sharp, shooting sensation that merged every now and then . . . and a point which kept moving from one place to another. This point I identified as the *pain* . . . As I kept up this awareness exercise I found I was bearing the pain quite well and even had some awareness left over for other sensations in other parts of my body. For the first time in my life I was experiencing pain without suffering.

If you are not sitting cross-legged during this exercise, it is not likely that the physical pain you experience will be as acute as the one I experienced. But some pain you will inevitably experience at the beginning, until your body has become accustomed to remaining perfectly still. Deal with the pain through awareness. And when your body finally does become still you will have a rich reward in the quiet bliss that this stillness will bring you.

The temptation to scratch is another frequent temptation with beginners. That is because, as their awareness of their body sensations sharpens, they become aware of itching and pricking sensations that were there all along but were hidden to awareness because of the psychophysical hardening that most of us submit our bodies to and because of the grossness of their awareness. While you are going through this *itching* stage, you will have to remain perfectly still and become aware of each itching sensation and stay with that awareness till the itching disappears—and resist the temptation to deal with the itching by scratching!

Exercise 9: Body Prayer

Here is another *devotional* variant of the body sensation exercises:

First quiet yourself through the awareness of sensations in various parts of your body . . . Sharpen your awareness by picking up even the subtlest sensations, not just the gross and evident ones . . .

Now very gently move your hands and fingers so that your hands come to rest on your lap, palms facing upward, fingers joined together . . . The movement must be very, very slow . . . like the opening of the petals of a flower . . . And while the movement is going on, be aware of each part of it . . .

Once your hands are resting on your lap, palms facing upward, become aware of the sensations in the palms . . . Then become aware of the gesture itself: this is a gesture of prayer to God that is common to most cultures and religions. What meaning does this gesture have for you? What are you saying to God through it? Say it without words, merely identifying with the gesture . . .

This kind of nonverbal communication through gesture that you have just practiced is the kind that can be practiced in a group and does not require any major change in your posture. It may give you some taste of the kind of prayer you can make with your body.

Here are some exercises you could try in the privacy of your room, where you can express yourself freely with your body without the embarrassment of being seen by others:

Stand erect with your hands hanging loosely at your sides. Become aware that you are in the presence of God . . .

Now find some way of expressing to him, through gestures, the following sentiment: *"My God, I offer myself to you"* . . . Make this gesture very slowly (remember the petals of a flower opening), being fully aware of your movements and making sure that the movements and the gestures express your sentiment . . .

Here is one way of expressing the attitude of self-offering: Raise your hands very slowly till they are stretched out in front of you, your arms parallel to the floor . . . Now gently turn your hands so that the palms face upward, fingers joined together and outstretched . . . Now raise your head very slowly till you are looking up to heaven . . . If your eyes are closed, open your eyes now with the same slowness . . . Gaze up at God . . .

Hold this gesture for a minute . . . Now let your hands drop gently back to their original position and let your head come down again till it faces the horizon . . . Pause for a moment to take in the prayer of offering you have just made nonverbally . . . And begin the rite once again . . .

Perform this rite three or four times . . . or as often as you find devotion in performing it . . .

An alternative to the gesture I have just suggested to express self-offering: Raise your hands as suggested above and turn your palms upward, fingers joined together and outstretched . . . Now bring your palms together to form a cup or chalice . . . Slowly bring this cup close to your chest . . . Then gently raise your head heavenward as suggested above . . . Hold this position for a minute.

Another sample, this one to express desire for God or welcome to him or to the whole of creation: Raise your hands and arms till they are stretched out in front of you, parallel to the floor . . . Now open them out wide in the form of an embrace . . . Look longingly toward the horizon . . .

Hold this posture for a minute, then revert to your original posture, rest for a moment to take in the prayer you have just made. Then repeat the gesture as often as it is meaningful to you . . .

The gestures I have suggested in the exercise are merely samples. Invent your own gestures to express love . . . praise . . . adoration . . .

Or act out something you want to say to God. Do it slowly and as gracefully as possible, so that it becomes a slow-moving ritual dance . . .

If you feel helpless, for instance, and are unable to pray, if you find yourself without resources, express this by stripping yourself of your clothes, prostrating yourself on the ground and spreading your arms out in the form of a cross . . . mutely expecting God to pour down his graces on your prostrate form . . .

When you pray with your body you give power and *body* to your prayer. This is particularly needed at the times when you feel unable to pray, when your mind is distracted, your heart has turned to stone, and your spirit seems dead. Then try to stand in the presence of God in a very devout way, hands devoutly joined in front of you, eyes looking at him supplicatingly . . . Some of this devotion you are expressing through your body is likely to seep through into your spirit, and after a while you may find it much easier to pray.

People sometimes run into difficulty in their prayer because they fail to attend to their body in prayer; they fail to take their bodies along with them into the holy temple of God. You say you are standing or sitting in the presence of the Risen Lord, but you are carelessly slouched in your chair or you are standing in a very slovenly fashion . . . You are obviously still not gripped by the

living presence of the Lord. If you were turning to him fully I
would notice some of this in your body.

I shall end this chapter with yet another exercise that you can
practice in a group, like the exercise connected with the palms of
your hands:

> Close your eyes. Quieten yourself through one of the aware-
> ness exercises . . .
>
> Now slowly raise your face upward toward God . . . Let
> your eyes continue to be closed . . . What are you saying to
> God through your upturned face? Stay with that sentiment or
> that communication for a few moments . . . Then become as
> fully aware as possible of the position of your face . . . of the
> sensations on your face . . .
>
> After a few moments ask yourself once again what you are
> expressing to God through your upturned face and stay with
> that for a while . . .

Exercise 10: The Touch of God

This is a *devotional* variant to the exercises on body sensations that
you will find helpful if you have reservations about calling the
body sensation exercises true prayer or contemplation:

> Repeat one of the body sensation exercises . . . Take some
> time to experience as many and as subtle sensations as you can
> in various parts of your body . . .
>
> Now make the reflection: Every sensation I feel, no matter
> how light and subtle, is the result of a biochemical reaction that
> could not exist except for God's almighty power . . . Feel
> God's power at work in the production of every single sensa-
> tion . . .
>
> Feel him touching you in each of those sensations that he is
> producing . . . Feel the touch of God in different parts of
> your body: rough, smooth, pleasurable, painful . . .

People who are desirous of the experience of God and concerned that they do not as yet have it ask me anxiously how they
can acquire this experience of God. The experience of God need
not be something sensational or out of the ordinary. There is, no
doubt, an experience of God that is different from the ordinary
run of experiences that we are accustomed to. There is the deep
silence that I spoke of earlier, the glowing darkness, the emptiness that brings fulfillment. There are sudden, unaccountable
flashes of eternity or of the infinite that come to us when we least
expect them, in the midst of our work or play.

There is the sense of being taken out of ourselves when we are
exposed to beauty or to love . . . We rarely think of these experiences as sensational or out of the ordinary. We barely turn to
them. We do not recognize them for what they are and we continue to search for the great *experience of God* that will transform
our lives.

One needs to do so little, really, to *experience God.* All one needs
to do is quieten oneself, become still—and become aware of the
feel of your hand. Be aware of the sensations in your hand . . .
There you have God, living and working in you, touching you,
intensely near you . . . Feel him. Experience him!

Most people look upon an experience like this as far too pedes-
trian. Surely there is more to the experience of God than just the
simple feel of the sensations of one's right hand! They are like the
Jews who were straining their eyes toward the future in expectation of a glorious, sensational Messiah, while all along the Messiah was beside them in the form of a man called Jesus of Nazareth.

We forget all too easily that one of the big lessons of the
incarnation is that God is found in the ordinary. You wish to see
God? Look at the face of the man next to you. You want to hear
him? Listen to the cry of a baby, the loud laughter at a party, the
wind rustling in the trees. You want to feel him? Stretch your
hand out and hold someone. Or touch the chair you are sitting on
or this book that you are reading. Or just quieten yourself, be-

come aware of the sensations in your body, sense his almighty power at work in you and feel how near he is to you. Emmanuel. God with us.

Exercise 11:   Sounds

If I am not careful to choose a quiet place for my Contemplation Groups some of the members of the group invariably complain about the sounds around them. The traffic in the street. The blare of a radio. A door banging. A telephone bell ringing. All of these sounds seem to intrude upon their quiet and peacefulness and to distract them.

Some sounds are considered to foster silence and prayer. Listen to the sound of a church bell toward dusk, for instance, or the sound of the birds in the early morning, or the sound of an organ playing softly in a vast church. No complaint there! Yet there is no sound, except a sound that is so loud as to cause damage to your eardrums, that need disturb your silence and peacefulness. If you learn to take all the sounds that surround you into your contemplation (supposing that they do intrude on your awareness while you are in contemplation), you will discover that there is a deep silence in the heart of all sounds. That is why I like to hold my prayer group sessions in places that are not entirely silent. A room above a busy street suits my purpose admirably.

Here is an exercise that will help you to find contemplation in the sounds around you:

Close your eyes. Block your ears with your thumbs. Cover your eyes with the palms of your hands.

You will now hear none of the sounds around you. Listen to the sound of your breathing.

After ten full breaths, gently bring your hands to rest on your lap. Let your eyes remain closed. Listen attentively now to all the sounds around you—to as many of them as possible, the

big sounds, the small ones; the ones that are near, the ones that
are distant . . .

After a while, listen to these sounds without identifying them
(sound of footsteps, clock ticking, sound of traffic . . .). Listen to the whole world of sound around you as one whole . . .

Sounds are distracting when you attempt to run away from
them, when you attempt to push them out of your consciousness,
when you protest that they have no right to be there. In this last
instance they are both distracting and irritating. If you just accept
them and become aware of them you will find them not a source
of distraction and irritation but a means for attaining silence. You
will learn through experience how relaxing this exercise is.

It is also good contemplation. You may apply to it the theory I
gave you about developing the Heart within you that grasps God.
Instead of occupying your mind with the awareness of body sensations, you can occupy it with the awareness of the sounds
around you while your mystical mind, your Heart, gradually un-
folds and begins to attend to God.

If this theory, however, does not please you, here is a means of
making the contemplation in this exercise more explicit:

Listen to all the sounds around you as indicated in the exercise above . . .

Make sure you turn even to the smallest sounds. One sound
is frequently composed of many other sounds . . . it has vari-
ations in pitch and intensity . . . See how many of these nu-
ances you can pick up . . .

Now become aware, not so much of the sounds around you,
as of your act of hearing . . .

What do you feel when you realize that you have the faculty
of hearing? Gratitude . . . praise . . . joy . . . love . . . ?

Return now to the world of sounds . . . and keep alternat-
ing from awareness of sound to awareness of your hearing
activity . . .

Now reflect that each sound is produced and sustained by

God's almighty power . . . God is *sounding* all around you
. . . Rest in this world of sounds . . . Rest in God.

The ability to see God's activity in everything was something
typical of the Hebrew mentality we find in the Bible. Where we
seem to dwell almost exclusively on secondary causes, the
Hebrews seemed to dwell almost exclusively on the Primary
Cause. Were their armies defeated in battle? It was God who
defeated them, not the ineptness of their generals! Did it rain? It
was God who made the rain fall. Were their crops destroyed by
locusts? It was God who sent the locusts. Even more daringly they
would speak of God hardening the hearts of wicked men!

Their view of reality was, admittedly, partial. They seemed to
ignore secondary causes entirely. Our modern view of reality is
equally, and more grossly, partial, for we seem to ignore the
Primary Cause entirely. Has your headache disappeared? Where
the Hebrew would have said, *"God cured you,"* we say, *"Leave God
out of this, the aspirin tablet cured you."* The reality is that it was God
who cured you through the aspirin tablet, of course. We have,
however, all but lost our sense of the Infinite operating within our
lives. We no longer sense God guiding us to our destiny through
our rulers, God healing us of our emotional wounds through our
counselors, God bringing us health through our physicians, God
shaping every event that we meet, God sending every person who
enters our life, God producing the rain, God playing about us in
the breeze and touching us in every sensation we feel and producing sounds all around us so that they shall be registered on
our eardrums and we shall hear him!

A pleasant addition to this exercise is to have the group or the
group leader chant an antiphon in a soft voice. Chanting the
Sanskrit word *om* is a great help. The idea is to chant a line or a
syllable, then pause in silence for a while, then chant again. You
may even try this if you are contemplating alone. The important
thing is to listen not just to the sound of the chanting but also to
the silence that follows each line or word that you chant.

I frequently introduce some chanting into silent group contemplation at regular intervals. It deepens the silence if the group knows how to listen. A similar effect can be attained by striking a pleasant-sounding gong at regular intervals. Strike the gong, listen to the resonance, listen to the sound die away, listen to the silence that follows.

Exercise 12:   Concentration

This is an exercise in pure awareness:

Choose one sense object for a basic object of attention. I suggest you choose either the sensations in one part of your body *or* your breathing *or* the sounds around you.

Focus your attention on this object, but do so in such a way that if your attention shifts to something else you are immediately aware of the shift.

Let us suppose you have chosen for your basic object of attention your breathing. Well, then, concentrate on your breathing . . . It is quite likely that after a while your attention will move to something else—a thought, a sound, a feeling . . . Now, provided you are aware of this shift of attention to something else, this shift is not to be counted as a distraction. It is important, however, that you be aware of the shift while the shift is taking place, or immediately after it has taken place. Count it a distraction only if you become aware of the shift long after it has taken place.

Suppose you choose breathing as your basic object of attention. Then your exercise will possibly go something like this (I am describing your awareness): *I am breathing . . . I am breathing . . . Now I am thinking . . . thinking . . . thinking . . . Now I am listening to a sound . . . listening . . . listening . . . Now I am irritated . . . irritated . . . Now I feel bored . . . bored . . . bored . . .*

In this exercise, the wandering of the mind is not considered a distraction provided you are *aware* that your mind is wandering, that your attention is shifting to some other object . . . Once you have become aware of this shift, stay with the new object (thinking, listening, feeling . . .) for a while, then return to the basic object of your attention (breathing) . . .

Your skill in self-awareness may become so great that you will become aware not only of the shift of your attention onto some object, but even of the desire to shift, the impulse in you to shift onto something else. As when you want to move your hand, you will first become conscious of the desire arising within you to move the hand, your consent to this desire, your carrying out of this desire, the very first stirring of your hand . . .

All of these activities are performed in an infinitesimal fraction of a second, and so we find it impossible to distinguish one from the other until the silence and stillness within us has become almost total and our awareness has acquired razor-edge sharpness.

Self-awareness is sometimes regarded as a form of selfishness and people are therefore urged to *forget* themselves and move out to others. To understand how disastrous this kind of advice can be, all you have to do is listen to the recorded interview of a well-intentioned, outgoing, but unaware counselor with his client. When this good counselor is not aware of what is going on within himself, he is certainly not going to be aware of what is going on deep down within his client or what is going on in the interchange between him and his client. He is then much less effective in helping his client and even in danger of doing positive harm.

Self-awareness is a powerful means for increasing in love of God and of neighbor. The self-awareness heightens the love. The love, when it is genuine, fosters deeper self-awareness.

Do not go in search of abstruse means for developing your self-awareness. Begin with humble things like the awareness of the feel of your body or awareness of the things around you and then move on to exercises like the ones I have suggested here and it won't be long before you notice the fruits of peacefulness and love that heightened self-awareness brings with it.

Exercise 13:   Finding God in All Things

This is a recapitulation of most of the previous exercises:

Do any of the awareness exercises that have preceded.

Take your body sensation, for instance, as the focus of your attention . . . Observe not only the sensations that yield themselves readily to your awareness, the grosser sensations, but also the subtler ones . . . If possible, do not give the sensations any names (burning, numbness, pricking, itching, cold . . .). Just feel the sensations without putting a label on them . . .

Do the same with sounds . . . Capture as many of them as possible . . . Do not try to identify the sources of the sounds . . . Listen to the sounds without putting a label on them . . .

As you proceed with this exercise you will notice a great peacefulness coming upon you, a deep silence . . . Now become aware, briefly, of this peacefulness and silence . . .

Feel how good it is to be here now. To have nothing to do. To just be.

Be.

For those who are more devotionally inclined:

Do the previous exercise until you sense the peacefulness that comes with it . . .

Become aware, for a brief while, of that peacefulness and silence . . .

Now express yourself to God nonverbally. Imagine that you are dumb and you can only communicate with your eyes and your breathing. Say to the Lord, nonverbally, *"Lord, it is good to be here with you."*

Or, do not *communicate* with the Lord at all. Just rest in his presence.

Also, for the devotionally inclined, a rudimentary exercise in *finding God in all things:*

> Return to the world of the senses. Become as keenly aware as possible of the air you breathe . . . of the sounds around you . . . of the sensations you feel in your body . . .
> *Sense* God in the air, the sounds, the sensations . . .
> Rest in this whole world of the senses. Rest in God . . .
> Surrender to this whole world of the senses (sounds, tactile sensations, colors . . .) . . . Surrender to God . . .

Exercise 14:   Awareness of the Other

So far, all the exercises you have done were based on awareness of the self, and awareness of God through the self. That is because for you there is no reality that is closer to God than your self. You will experience nothing closer to God than your self. Saint Augustine would therefore rightly insist that we must restore man to himself so that he can make of himself a stepping-stone to God. God is the very ground of my being, the Self of my self, and I cannot go deep into my self without coming in touch with him.

The awareness of self is also a means for developing awareness of the other. It is only inasmuch as I am attuned to my own feelings that I am able to be aware of the feelings of others. It is only inasmuch as I am aware of my reactions to others that I am able to go out to them in love, without doing them any harm. When I become sensitively aware of my self I also develop a refined awareness of my brother. If I am having difficulty being aware of the reality nearest to me, my self, how can I avoid having difficulty being aware of God and my brother?

The exercise in awareness of the other that I am going to propose now does not deal with awareness of our fellow men as you probably expect. I am going to take something that is easier: the awareness of the rest of creation. From that you can then graduate to man. In this exercise I want you to develop an attitude of reverence and respect for all inanimate creation, for all the objects that surround you. Some of the great mystics tell us that when they reach the stage of illumination they become mysteriously filled with a sense of deep reverence. Reverence for God, reverence for life in all its forms, reverence for inanimate creation too. And they tend to personalize the whole of creation. They no longer treat persons as things. They no longer treat things as things—it is as if even things have become persons to them—and as a result of this their respect and love for persons becomes heightened.

Francis of Assisi was one such mystic. He recognized in the sun, the moon, the stars, the trees, the birds, the animals, his brothers and sisters. They were members of his family and he would talk to them lovingly. Saint Anthony of Padua went to the extent of preaching a sermon to fish! Very foolish, of course, from our rationalist point of view. Profoundly wise and personalizing and sanctifying from the mystical point of view.

I should like you to experience some of this for yourself rather than have you just read about it. Hence this exercise. But for this you will have to temporarily put aside your *adult* prejudices and become like a little child that will talk to its doll in all seriousness or like Francis of Assisi who would do the same with the sun and moon and animals. If you become a little child, at least temporarily, you might discover a kingdom of heaven—and learn secrets that God ordinarily hides from the wise and prudent.

Choose some object that you use frequently: a pen, a cup
. . . It should be an object that you can easily hold in your
hands . . .

Let the object rest on the palms of your outstretched hands.
Now close your eyes and get the feel of it on your palms . . .
Become as fully aware of it as possible. First become aware of
its weight . . . then of the sensation it produces on your
palms . . .

Now explore it with your fingers or with both your hands. It
is important that you do this gently and reverently. Explore its
roughness or smoothness, its hardness or softness, its warmth
or coldness . . . Now touch it to other parts of your body and
see if it feels different. Touch it to your lips . . . your cheeks
. . . your forehead . . . the back of your hand . . .

You have become acquainted with your object through your
sense of touch . . . Now become acquainted with it, become
aware of it through your sense of sight. Open your eyes and
look at it from different angles . . . See every possible detail
in it: its colors, its form, its various parts . . .

Smell it . . . taste it, if possible . . . hear it, by placing it
close to your ear . . .

Now gently place the object in front of you or on your lap
and speak to it . . . Begin by asking it questions about itself
. . . its life, its origins, its future . . . And listen while it un-
folds to you the secret of its being and of its destiny . . .
Listen while it explains to you what existence means to it . . .

Your object has some hidden wisdom to reveal to you about
yourself . . . Ask for this and listen to what it has to say . . .
There is something that you can give this object . . . What is
it? What does it want from you? . . .

Now place yourself and this object in the presence of Jesus
Christ, the Word of God, in whom and for whom everything
was made. Listen to what he has to say to you and to the object
. . . What do the two of you say in response? . . .

Now look at your object once more . . . Has your attitude

toward it changed? . . . Is there any change in your attitude toward the other objects around you . . .

PERSONAL BENEFITS FROM AWARENESS

When you first start out on the type of contemplation proposed in the exercises that have preceded, you are likely to have misgivings regarding the value of these exercises. They seem to be neither meditation nor prayer in the traditional sense of the words. If prayer is understood as *speaking with God*, there is very little or no speaking at all here. If meditation is taken to mean reflection, lights and insights, resolutions, then there is hardly any scope for meditation in these exercises.

You come away from these exercises with nothing concrete to show for all the effort you put into them. Nothing you can write about in your spiritual diary—at least not at the beginning and, maybe, not ever. You will frequently come away with the uneasy feeling that you have done nothing and achieved nothing. This form of prayer is particularly painful to the young and to those who set great store by achievement—people to whom effort is more important than just being.

I vividly remember one young person who seemed to attain nothing from these exercises. He found it very frustrating to have to sit down motionless and expose himself to a blank, even though he admitted that he simply could not think or use his mind in any other way while he was at prayer. He would spend most of the time that he dedicated to these exercises in dealing with distractions—generally unsuccessfully—and he pleaded with me to offer him something that would make the time and effort he expended in prayer seem more worth his while. He fortunately persevered in these seemingly frustrating exercises and after some six months he came to report to me that he was drawing immense benefit from them—far more than he had ever attained from his former prayers and meditations and lights and resolutions. What had happened? He was certainly finding a greater peace in these exercises. His distractions had not diminished. He was finding the exercises as frustrating as before. Nothing had changed in the exercises. What had changed was his life! This constant, painful, distraction-ridden attempt he was making day after day to expose himself to what seemed to be nothingness and emptiness, to attempt to just quieten his mind and attain some sort of silence through concentration on body sensations or breathing or sounds, was bringing him a new power in his daily living that he hadn't noticed there before—and power in so great a measure that its presence in his life was unmistakable.

This is one of the major benefits of this form of prayer: a change in oneself that seems effortless. All the virtues you formerly tried to attain through the exercise of your *will power* seem to come to you effortlessly now—sincerity, simplicity, kindliness, patience . . . Addictions seem to drop off without the need for resolutions and effort on one's part: thing addictions like smoking and the excessive use of alcohol, person addictions like infatuations and overdependency.

When this happens to you, you will know that the time investment you made in these exercises is yielding rich dividends.

GROUP BENEFITS OF AWARENESS

If you make these exercises in a group, you will also notice the group benefits that they bring. The highest of these benefits is an increase of love among the members of the group. Many attempts are being made today, and very laudable ones, to bring about a greater union of hearts among members of religious communities and families through dialogue, group sharing, and group encounter. There is an additional way of achieving this result: through group contemplation, when all the members of the group sit together for at least half an hour each day, preferably in a circle (I do not know why this helps, but it does) in total silence. It is important that the silence be not just external—no physical movements in the room, no fidgeting, no verbalization of prayer —but internal too, namely, that the group members strive to create a silence of words and thoughts within themselves through exercises similar to the ones suggested so far.

One married man told me that he and his wife spend an hour each morning in this form of contemplation facing each other with eyes closed and, as a result, after each hour they experience a union of hearts and a love for each other that far exceeds anything they had ever known before, even when they were romantically in love with each other. I must add that these two have become experts in the art of contemplation and of silencing the mind.

One priest who made a thirty-day retreat under me with a group of forty other priests who were totally unknown to him even by name told me, at the end of the retreat, that he had felt closer to this group than to any other group he had ever lived with in all his life. All that had happened during the retreat to make him feel this oneness with the group was that the group met each night for some forty-five minutes of common contemplation in complete silence.

Silence, when it is deep, can unite. Words can sometimes be used to impede communication! One retreat master who conducts retreats very similar to Zen retreats, at which the participants spend hours together in total silence and in emptying the mind of all thought content, told me that he always gets his retreatants to practice their contemplation together in a hall. The reason: it helped enormously to bring all these people—as many as eighty of them, generally total strangers to one another— together and give them a deep sense of union with one another.

CONTEMPLATION EASIER IN A GROUP

You will probably find it easier to achieve concentration and to practice these exercises profitably if you make them together with a group of people who are also attempting to achieve the silence that these exercises bring.

It is important that all the members of the group be making a serious attempt to practice this form of contemplation. Laziness or mental lassitude on the part of one person will serve as a drag on the others, just as the efforts of some "contemplatives" in the group will serve as an enormous help to others. Again and again, retreatants have told me what a difference it makes to their contemplation when they make it together with a group rather than alone in their rooms. This is not an absolutely universal rule, of course, but I was certainly struck by the fact that when one or other of the retreatants at the Buddhist retreat I attended was finding it particularly hard to concentrate, our retreat master would invite him to sit close to him—and that invariably seemed to help!

Is there some kind of unconscious communication that goes on when individuals achieve deep silence in physical proximity to one another? Or are "vibrations" generated through this exercise that have a beneficial effect on those who are close enough to be exposed to these vibrations? This was the theory of our Buddhist retreat master. He also earnestly recommended another practice that I have found beneficial: that, as far as possible, you make your contemplation each time in the same place, the same corner, a corner or a room that is reserved for this purpose only, or that you make it in a place that is used by others for prayer and contemplation. The reason: once again, according to him, the good vibrations that were generated through the practice of contemplation and that seemed to persist in that place long after the contemplation was over. Whether the reason is an accurate one or not, I know from my own and others' experience that it helps to pray in "sacred" places that have been sanctified by the frequent practice of contemplation.

THE SPECIAL VALUE OF BODY AWARENESS

I have frequently suggested that you choose awareness of your breathing or of sounds or of body sensations for your contemplation. Are all of these of equal value? In my opinion, awareness of body sensations has an advantage over the awareness of sounds and of breathing. In addition to the spiritual benefits it brings, there are many psychological benefits that come to the person who practices this kind of awareness until there is no part of his body that does not yield sensations to his awareness.

There is a very close connection between the body and the psyche and any harm done to one seems to affect the other. Conversely, any increase in the health of one seems to have a beneficial effect on the other. When your awareness of your body becomes so sharp that every part of it becomes alive with sensations, a great loosening of tensions takes place—physical and emotional tensions. And so I have known people to be released from psychosomatic illnesses like asthma and migraine headaches, and also from emotional hang-ups like resentments and neurotic fears, through the steady practice of body sensations awareness.

Sometimes this exercise will result in an opening up of the unconscious and so you may be flooded with strong feelings and fantasies connected with repressed material, generally feelings and fantasies connected with sex and anger. There is really no danger here at all, provided you continue with your awareness exercise and give no importance or attention to the fantasies and feelings. Only make sure, as I said earlier, that you do not spend many hours at a stretch in breathing awareness unless there is a competent guide available.

So if you wish to seriously and systematically undertake the practice of these exercises, I recommend that you begin with the awareness of breathing and sounds for a few minutes at the beginning of each exercise and then move on to the awareness of body sensations, giving this latter the greater importance and moving over all the parts of your body until the whole of your body becomes one teeming mass of sensations. Then rest in the awareness of your body as a whole until you find you are getting distracted and need to move from one part to the other again. This will bring you the spiritual benefits of opening your Heart to the divine, plus the benefits to psyche and body that go with this exercise.

A final word of encouragement: The peace and joy that I have promised you as a reward for faithfully practicing these exercises is a sentiment that you are probably not accustomed to—something that at the beginning is so subtle that it hardly seems like a feeling or an emotion at all. If you are not aware of this, you might become discouraged too easily.

The enjoyment of this peace and joy is an acquired taste. When a child is told that beer is enjoyable he is likely to approach his glass of beer with his own experience of what *enjoyable* means and is then surprised and disappointed that the beer contains none of the sweetness that he gets from his soft drinks. He was told that beer would be *enjoyable*—his concept of enjoyable was limited to *sweet.* Do not approach the exercise of contemplation with any preconceived notions at all. Approach it with a readiness to discover new experiences (that initially may not even seem like "experience" at all) and to acquire brand-new tastes.

FANTASY

Exercise 15: There and Here

There is an unsuspected and untapped source of power and life in our fantasy. I want to show this to you through an experiment before I introduce you to the use of fantasy in contemplation.

Close your eyes. Take up a restful posture. Quieten yourself for a while through one of the awareness exercises. For all fantasy work it is important that your mind be quiet and rested and peaceful . . .

Now withdraw in fantasy to some place in which you experienced happiness in the past . . . Once you have chosen the place, spend some time recapturing every detail of the place . . . Use each one of your imaginative *senses* for this: see the objects in that place, the colors, hear every sound again, touch and taste and smell if that is possible, till the place becomes as vividly present as possible to you . . .

What are you doing? . . . What are you feeling? . . .

After being in this place for some five minutes come back to the present, to your existence in this room in which we are now . . . Notice as many details of your situation here as possible . . . Notice, especially, what you are feeling here . . . Stay with this for some three minutes . . .

Now return to the place to which you had withdrawn in fantasy . . . What do you feel now? . . . Is there any change in the place or in your feelings? . . .

Return again to this room . . . and keep moving back and forth, between that place and this room, noticing each time what you are feeling and any change in feelings that occurs in you . . .

After a few minutes I shall ask you to open your eyes and end the experiment, and to share your experience with us if you wish.

In the sharing that follows this exercise most people tell me they feel refreshed and strengthened. They retire in fantasy to some place where they have experienced love or joy or deep peace and silence in the past . . . When they recapture the scene in their imagination they are also able to recapture the emotions that they originally experienced in that scene.

The return to the room where they actually are often proves painful . . . But as they keep moving back and forth between the place of their fantasy and the room, they bring back with them from the *fantasy place* a good deal of the positive emotion they experienced there. They come back refreshed and strengthened. And, strange as it may seem, their perception of present reality becomes sharpened. Far from serving as an escape from reality, as many people fear when they withdraw into their fantasy world, this withdrawal has helped them to plunge more deeply into present reality—to perceive it better and to come to grips with it with renewed vigor.

The next time you feel tired and bored, try this experiment and see what it does for you. You may be one of those people who have rarely used their power of fantasy and find it difficult in the beginning to imagine anything vividly, and so you will need some practice before you can get the full benefits of this invigorating exercise. But if you persevere, you will eventually succeed.

Make sure, when you try this experiment next, that you genuinely fantasize and not just remember the scene or event. The difference between fantasy and memory is that in fantasy I actually relive the event I remember; I am no longer conscious of my present surroundings. As far as my mind and consciousness is concerned, I am actually in my fantasy place. Thus, if I am fantasizing a scene on the seashore, I imagine that I hear once again the roar of the waves, I feel again the sun beating on my bare back, I feel the touch of the hot sand under my feet . . . and, as a result, I experience, once again, all the feelings that I had when that scene first took place.

Formerly I would accept the statement of retreatants who said to me, *"I cannot pray with my imagination . . . I have a very poor imagination."* And I would advise them to use some other form of prayer. Today I have become convinced that with a little practice everyone can develop his power to fantasize and thus acquire untold emotional and spiritual riches.

If you think you are not able to use your fantasy at all, try this. Look at some object in front of you for a while. Now close your eyes and see if you can visualize that object mentally. Notice how many details you are able to capture. Then open your eyes and look at the object again and notice what it is you missed in your mental image. Close your eyes again and see how many details of your object you can recapture, how vividly you can see it . . . You can try something similar with your imaginative sense of hearing. Listen to a few bars of music played on a recorder . . . recapture them mentally . . . replay the tape and notice what you missed . . . It is thus that you will gradually develop your power to fantasize.

Let us now *spiritualize* the experiment I gave you above and get you to draw some spiritual profit from it:

Close your eyes and quieten yourself for a while . . .

Now withdraw in fantasy to any place where you experienced God in the past . . .

Follow the same procedure I suggested in the previous experiment . . . move to and from that place and this one . . . See if you can recapture something of the spiritual experience you had in the past and bring with you into the present some of the spiritual power that that experience gave you.

To fantasize successfully and draw the maximum profit from these exercises, you must be in a state of deep inner solitude.

Then your fantasies become vivid. Ideally they should be almost as vivid as the reality of the sense world.

You need not fear that these exercises will make you an escapist or a daydreamer. Daydreams are dangerous only when the dreamer cannot distinguish between sense reality and fantasy reality or when he has no power to turn his dreams off and on at will. Provided you retain this power, you can move into these exercises without any fear.

Exercise 16:   A Place for Prayer

One of the finest helps to our prayer is a place that is conducive to prayer. I spoke above of places that contain good "vibrations." Quite apart from this, you may have noticed what a beautiful sunrise or sunset does to your recollectedness and your prayer. Or the twinkling of the stars at night when they shine out brightly against a black sky. Or the moonlight shining brightly through the trees.

Closeness to nature helps most people pray—and helps them substantially. People have their preferences, of course: the seashore with the sound of the waves beating against the sand, or a quietly flowing river, or the stillness and beautiful surroundings of a lake, or the peace of a mountaintop . . . Has it ever occurred to you that Jesus, that master in the art of prayer, would take the trouble to walk up a hill in order to pray? Like all great contemplatives he was aware that the place in which we pray has an influence on the quality of our prayer.

Most of us, unfortunately, live in surroundings that cut us off from nature, and the places we are forced to choose for prayer are, alas, drab and hardly conducive to lifting our spirits to God. All the more reason to expose ourselves long and lovingly to places that help us to pray whenever we get the chance. Take time out to gaze at and drink in the atmosphere of the starry or moonlit night or the seashore or the mountaintop or whatever. You can then carry this around with you in your heart, and even though you may be far from these places geographically, you will have them vividly etched in your memory and will be able to return to them in fantasy.

Try this right now:

> After some time spent in quietening yourself, withdraw in fantasy to some place that is likely to foster prayer for you: a seashore, riverbank, mountaintop, a silent church, a terrace that gives onto the starry sky, a garden flooded by the light of the moon . . .
>
> See the place as vividly as possible . . . All the colors . . . Hear all the sounds (the waves, the wind in the trees, the insects at night . . .).
>
> Now raise your heart to God and say something to him.

Those of you who are familiar with the Spiritual Exercises of Saint Ignatius of Loyola will recall what is commonly called the "composition of place." Ignatius recommends that we reconstruct the place where the scene we are about to contemplate occurred. What he really speaks of, however, in the original Spanish text, is not a *composition of place*, but a *composition, seeing the place.* In other words, it is not the place that you compose but yourself when you see it in fantasy. If you have succeeded in the above exercise, you will know exactly what Ignatius is talking about.

And you will have a peace center in your heart to which you can always retire when you are in need of quiet and solitude, even though you are externally in the marketplace or on a crowded train.

Exercise 17:   The Return to Galilee

When lovers have quarreled and want to come together again, it is a great help to remember the happy times they spent together in the past. God was constantly reminding the Hebrews through the prophets of the honeymoon he had with his people when he took Israel for his bride in the desert, while now, in the land of milk and honey, Israel goes after false lovers because she has forgotten the days of her honeymoon with God.

In times of spiritual crisis it is good to follow the advice of the Risen Lord to his dejected apostles: *"Return to Galilee."* Return to the joyful days spent in the company of the Lord. Return—and you will find him again. And probably find him in a new way as the Apostles did. But there is no need to wait for days of crisis in order to do this. If we did this frequently enough we might be able to avoid those crises.

> Return in imagination to some scene where you experienced God's goodness and God's love for you . . . in any form . . . Stay with it and take in God's love once again . . . Now come to the present and speak with God.
> Or return to an event when you felt very close to God . . . or when you felt intense spiritual joy and consolation . . .
> It is important that you relive the event in your imagination and not merely recollect it . . . Take all the time you need . . . This reliving will bring on again the feelings you experienced then: joy or intimacy or love . . . Then make sure that you do not run away from those feelings but *stay with them as long as you can* . . . Stay with them until you feel a sense of peacefulness and contentedness. Then return to the present . . . Speak with the Lord for a while and end the exercise.

The injunction about staying with those pleasant feelings is important because, strange as it may seem, the tolerance of most people for positive feelings is small. They have a deep-rooted sense of worthlessness which makes them instinctively turn away from any but the most momentary exposure to pleasurable feelings—or they feel guilty about it, or unworthy, or whatever . . . Watch for this tendency in you and make sure you stay with the feelings that come up within you as you relive the times that you spent delightfully in the company of the Lord.

Some of the saints were in the habit of making a note of the mystical experiences they had. They would keep a kind of diary of their dealings with the Lord. I do not recommend lengthy accounts of your spiritual experiences. But if the experience has been a powerful one, a brief note may help you later on to return to Galilee . . .

One of the tragedies of our dealings with the Lord, as of our dealings with our friends and loved ones, is that we are all too prone to forget!

Exercise 18:   The Joyful Mysteries of Your Life

Each of us carries in his heart an album of lovely pictures of the past: memories of events that brought gladness to us. I want you now to open this album and recall as many of these events as you can . . .

If you have never done this exercise before, you are not likely to find many such events at the first try. But you will gradually discover more and more buried away in your past and you will enjoy unearthing them and reliving them in the presence of the Lord. What is more, when new events come to bring you happiness you will cherish the memory of them and not allow them to get lost easily and you will carry around with you an immense treasury into which you can dip any time you wish to bring new joy and vigor to your living.

I imagine this is what Mary did when she carefully placed away within her heart precious memories of the infancy of Christ, memories to which she would lovingly return.

Return to some scene in which you felt deeply loved . . . How was this love shown to you? In words, looks, gestures, an act of service, a letter . . . ? Stay with the scene as long as you experience something of the joy that was yours when the event took place.

Return to some scene in which you felt joy . . . What produced this joy in you? Good news? . . . The fulfillment of some desire? . . . A scene of nature? . . . Recapture the original scene and the feelings that accompanied it . . . Stay as long as you can with these feelings . . .

This return to past scenes where you felt love and joy is one of the finest exercises I know for building up your psychological health. Many of us go through what one psychologist calls *peak experiences*. The pity is that when the experience actually takes place very few people have the capacity to surrender themselves to it. So they take in nothing of the experience, or very little. What they need to do is return to these experiences in fantasy and gradually take the experience in to the full. If you do this you will discover that, no matter how often you return to these experiences, you will always find in them a supply of nourishment. Their store never seems to get exhausted. They are a joy forever.

Make sure, however, that you do not return to these scenes and observe them from the outside, so to speak. They have to be relived, not observed. Act them out again, participate in them again. Let the fantasy be so vivid that it is as if the experience is actually taking place right now for the first time.

It won't be long before you experience the psychological value of this exercise and you acquire a new respect for fantasy as a source of life and energy. Fantasy is a very powerful tool for therapy and personality growth. If it is grounded on reality (when you fantasize events and scenes that have actually taken place), it has the same effect (pleasurable or painful) that reality itself has. If in the dim light of evening I see a friend coming toward me and I imagine him to be an enemy, all my reactions, psychological and physiological, will be the same as if the enemy were really there. If a thirsty man in the desert imagines he sees water, the effect on him will be exactly the same as the effect caused by his seeing real water. When you return to scenes where you felt love and joy, you will enjoy all the benefits that come from being exposed to love and joy . . . and the benefits are immense.

What is the spiritual significance of an exercise like this? In the first place, it breaks down the instinctive resistance that most people have to taking in love and joy. It increases their capacity for accepting love and welcoming joy into their lives. And so it increases their capacity for experiencing God and for opening their hearts to his love and to the happiness that the experience of him brings with it. He who will not allow himself to feel loved by the brother whom he sees, how will he allow himself to feel loved by the God he does not see?

In the second place, this exercise helps overcome the inherent sense of worthlessness, of unworthiness, of guilt, which is one of the principal obstacles that we place in the way of God's grace. In fact, the primary effect of God's grace when it enters our hearts is to make us feel intensely loved—and lovable. Exercises like this one prepare the soil for this grace by making us ready to accept the fact that we are lovable.

Here is another way of drawing spiritual benefit from this exercise:

Relive one of these scenes where you felt deeply loved or where you felt deep joy . . .
Seek and find the presence of the Lord in this scene . . .
In what form is he present?

This is one way of learning how to find God in all the events of your life, past and present.

Exercise 19: The Sorrowful Mysteries

People sometimes carry with them wounds from the past that still rankle within their hearts. With the passage of time the rankling may no longer be felt. But the harmful effect of the wound, if it has not healed, will persist.

For instance, a child will be overwhelmed with grief at the loss of his mother. The grief may be repressed and forgotten, but it continues to influence the life of this child now become a man. He may find it hard to get close to people for fear he will lose them, or he may not be able to take in the love people are offering him, or he gradually loses interest in life and people in general because emotionally he is still standing at his mother's grave, refusing to let her go, demanding a love from her which she can no longer give him.

Or you may have been deeply hurt by a friend. The hurt turns into resentment that keeps smoldering within you and gets mixed up with the very genuine love you have for him, so that, for some mysterious reason, the warmth goes out of your relationship with him.

Or something may have frightened you as a child, leaving an unpleasant memory and a propensity to fear and anxiety whenever you are faced with similar situations today.

Or you still carry around with you a feeling of guilt which you cannot get rid of and which serves no useful purpose.

It is helpful to return to the events that produced these negative feelings so as to drain them of any harmful effect they may be having on you today.

> Return to some scene in the past where you have felt pain or grief or hurt or fear or bitterness . . . Relive the event . . . But this time seek and find the presence of the Lord in it . . . In what way is he present there? . . .
>
> Or, imagine that the Lord himself is taking part in the event . . . What role is he playing? . . . Speak to him. Ask him the meaning of what is happening . . . Listen to what he says in reply . . .

It is a help to return to the event in imagination again and again until you are no longer affected by the negative feeling that is produced. Till you are able to let go of something that is causing you grief, to forgive someone who caused you pain, to face calmly what formerly caused you fright . . . Till you are able to relive the event in peace. Possibly even with feelings of joy and gratitude.

It is quite possible that in reliving these events as I have suggested you will begin to understand that the Lord himself has had a hand in bringing them about . . . It is also likely that your feelings of resentment or anger or bitterness will then turn against him. If this happens, it is important that you face these feelings and express them to the Lord without fear.

The Lord knows what is in your heart and nothing is achieved by hiding it. On the contrary, a frank expression of what you are feeling—even if you have to use bitter and hard words to express those feelings—will help to clear the atmosphere and will bring you closer to the Lord. It is wonderful that you should trust him so much, be so sure of his unconditional love for you that you can say hard things to him too! It is significant that Job in his sufferings said some very hard things to the Lord while his scandalized companions chided him and urged him to blame himself and not speak harshly about the Lord; but when the Lord finally appeared, he exonerated Job and expressed displeasure with his well-meaning but insincere friends!

Exercise 20: Release from Resentment

An unwillingness to forgive others for the real or imaginary wrongs they have done us is a poison that affects our health—physical, emotional, and spiritual—sometimes very deeply. You commonly hear people say, *"I can forgive, but I cannot forget,"* or *"I want to forgive but cannot."* What they really mean is they do not want to forgive. They want to hold on to the satisfaction they receive from nurturing the resentment. They simply do not want to let it go. They demand that the other person recognize his

guilt, that he apologize, that he make amends, that he be pun-
ished . . . as a condition for letting their resentment go and
releasing themselves from this poison that is eating into their
system.

Or, they may genuinely desire to let the resentment go, but it
continues to rankle within them because they have not had the
occasion to express it and *get it out of their system.* Often a genuine
desire is no substitute for this need to spit out all the anger and
resentment, at least in fantasy. There is no need for me to insist
that it is essential that our heart be entirely free from every trace
of resentment if we wish to progress in the art of contemplation.
Here is a simple way of ridding yourself of resentments that you
are nursing:

It generally helps, first of all, to get the resentment out of your
system. For this, imagine that you see the person you resent there
in front of you. Tell him of your resentment, express all your
anger to him as forcefully as you can. Do not balk at your choice
of words! It might also help to get the resentment out through
some physical exertion like pounding a mattress or pillow. People frequently collect resentments simply because they are too
fearful to be strong. They therefore turn in upon themselves the
firmness that they rightly needed to show to others. Forgiveness
and meekness, when practiced by people who are too fearful to
speak out and stand up for what they know is true, are not virtues
but a cover for cowardice.

After expressing all your resentment, but only *after,* look at the
whole incident that caused the resentment from the other person's point of view. Take his place and explain the whole thing.
How does the incident look when seen through his eyes? Realize
also that there is hardly any instance when someone slights or
attacks or hurts you as a result of malice. In most instances, even
supposing there was an intention to hurt, this was a result of
some deep-rooted unhappiness in the other person. Genuinely
happy people are not wicked. Moreover, in the vast majority of
instances, you personally are not the target of the other's attack.

He is seeking something (or someone else) in you that he has projected there. See if all of these considerations lead you to feel compassion for him rather than anger and resentment.

If all these efforts fail, it is quite likely that you are the type of person who unconsciously but actively works at collecting hurt feelings and resentments. It is strange but true that people actually set up situations where they will be slighted or offended and, having received what they set out to get, they give themselves the bad feeling they wanted all along! You will get over this tendency of yours if you neutralize your expectations of other people. In other words, keep your expectations, even express them to the other person if you wish, but leave him entirely free—realize that he is under absolutely no obligation whatsoever to live up to your expectations inasmuch as they are yours; and that will prevent you from giving yourself a bad feeling when the expectation is not met. Many people carry a chip on their shoulder when they go through life trying to relate to others with the implicit assumption *"If you truly loved me, you would* . . . (not criticize me, speak gently to me, remember my birthday, do the favor I am asking of you, etc., etc.)" It is very difficult for them to see that all these expectations of theirs have nothing to do with genuine love on the part of the other person.

Finally, to strengthen your decision to give up your resentment (that is the secret: do you really *want* to give it up and get on with life or with the relationship, or are you one of those who hug the resentment to themselves and complain that they *cannot* get rid of it?), do the following:

> Imagine you see Jesus on the Cross . . . Take all the time you need to picture him in vivid detail . . .
> Now go to the scene of your resentment . . . Stay with it for a while . . .
> Return to Jesus Crucified and gaze at him again . . .
> Keep alternating between the event that caused your resentment and the scene of Jesus on the Cross . . . until you notice

the resentment slipping away from you and feel the freedom and joy and lightheartedness that follow.

Do not be surprised if the resentful feelings return after a while. Keep dealing with them patiently. The sacrifice involved in renouncing negative feelings and becoming happy is too great for most people to make at one shot.

Exercise 21: The Empty Chair

I developed this exercise as a result of hearing the story of a priest who went to visit a patient in his home. He noticed an empty chair at the patient's bedside and asked what it was doing there. The patient said, "I had placed Jesus on that chair and was talking to him before you arrived . . . For years I found it extremely diffi-cult to pray until a friend explained to me that prayer was a matter of talking to Jesus. He told me to place an empty chair nearby, to imagine Jesus sitting on that chair, and to speak with him and listen to what he says to me in reply. I've had no difficulty praying ever since."

Some days later, so the story goes, the daughter of the patient came to the rectory to inform the priest that her father had died. She said, "I left him alone for a couple of hours. He seemed so peaceful. When I got back to the room I found him dead. I noticed a strange thing, though: his head was resting not on the bed but on a chair that was beside his bed."

Try this exercise yourself right now, even though at first it might seem childish to you:

Imagine you see Jesus sitting close to you. In doing this you are putting your imagination at the service of your faith. Jesus isn't here in the way you are imagining him, but he certainly is here and your imagination helps to make you aware of this.

Now speak to Jesus . . . If no one is around, speak out in a soft voice . . .

Listen to what Jesus says to you in reply . . . or what you
imagine him to say . . .

If you do not know what exactly to say to Jesus, narrate to him
all the events of the past day and give him your comment on each
of them. That is the difference between thinking and praying.
When we think, we generally talk to ourselves. When we pray, we
talk to God. Do not bother to imagine the details of his face and
clothing, etc. This might only prove distracting. Saint Teresa of
Ávila, who frequently prayed like this, says she could never imagine the face of Jesus . . . She only sensed his nearness as you
sense the nearness of someone whom you cannot see in a dark
room but whose presence there is clear to you.

This method of praying is one of the quickest means of experiencing the presence of Christ that I know of. Imagine that Jesus is
by your side all through the day. Speak with him frequently in the
midst of your occupations. Sometimes all you will be able to do is
glance at him, communicate with him without words . . . Saint
Teresa, who was a great advocate of this form of prayer, promises
that it will not be long before the person who prays in this way
will experience intense union with the Lord. People sometimes
ask me how they can *meet* the Risen Lord in their lives. I know of
no better way to suggest to them than this one.

Exercise 22:   Ignatian Contemplation

This is a form of fantasy prayer recommended by Saint Ignatius
of Loyola in his *Spiritual Exercises* and frequently used by many of
the saints. It consists in taking a scene from the life of Christ and
reliving it, taking part in it as if it were actually occurring and you
were a participant in the event. The best way of explaining to you
how this is done is to have you do it. I shall choose for this sample
exercise a passage from the gospel according to John:

After this, there was a Jewish religious feast, and Jesus went
to Jerusalem. There is in Jerusalem, by the Sheep Gate, a pool
with five porches. In the Hebrew language it is called Bethesda.
A large crowd of sick people were lying on the porches—the
blind, the lame, and the paralyzed . . .

(They were waiting for the water to move; for every now and
then an angel of the Lord went down into the pool and stirred
up the water. The first sick person to go down into the pool
after the water was stirred up was made well from whatever
disease he had.)

A man was there who had been sick for thirty-eight years.
Jesus saw him lying there, and he knew that the man had been
sick for such a long time; so he said to him, "Do you want to get
well?" The sick man answered, "Sir, I don't have anybody here
to put me in the pool when the water is stirred up; while I am
trying to get in, somebody else gets there first."

Jesus said to him, *"Get up, pick up your mat, and walk."* Immediately the man got well; he picked up his mat, and walked.

Quiet yourself for a while now, as a preparation for the
contemplation, through doing one of the awareness exercises . . .

Now imagine the pool called Bethesda . . . the five porches
. . . the pool . . . the surroundings . . . Take time out to
imagine the whole setting as vividly as possible, to *compose
yourself, seeing the place* . . . What kind of place is it? Clean or
dirty? Large or small? . . . Notice the architecture . . . Notice the weather . . .

Having prepared the stage, let the whole scene come to life
now. See the people near the pool . . . How many people are
there? . . . What sort of people? . . . How are they dressed?
. . . What are they doing? . . . What kind of illnesses are
they suffering from? . . . What are they saying? . . . What
are they doing? . . .

It is not enough for you to observe the whole scene from the

outside, as if it were a movie on the screen. You must participate in it . . . What are you doing there? . . . Why have you
come to this place? . . . What are your feelings as you survey
the scene and watch these people? . . . What are you doing?
. . . Do you speak to anyone? . . . To whom? . . .

Now notice the sick man whom the gospel passage speaks
about . . . Where in the crowd is he? . . . How is he
dressed? . . . Is there anyone with him? . . . Walk up to him
and speak with him . . . What do you say to him, or what do
you ask him? . . . What does he say in reply? . . . Spend
some time getting as many details of his life and his person as
possible . . . What sort of an impression does he make on
you? . . . What are your feelings while you converse with
him? . . .

As you are speaking with him you notice, out of the corner of
your eye, that Jesus has entered this place . . .

Watch all his actions and movements . . . Where does he
go? How does he act? . . . What do you think he is feeling? . . .

He is now coming toward you and the sick man . . . What
are you feeling now? . . . You step aside when you realize that
he wants to talk to the sick man . . . What is Jesus saying to
the man? . . . What does the man answer? . . . Listen to the
whole dialogue—fill in the sketchy account of the gospel . . .

Dwell especially on Jesus's question, "Do you want to get
well?" . . . Now listen to Jesus's command as he tells the man
to get up and walk . . . the first reaction of the man . . . his
attempt to get up . . . the miracle! Notice the reactions of the
man . . . notice Jesus's reactions . . . and your own . . .

Jesus now turns to you . . . He engages you in conversation
. . . Talk to him about the miracle that has just taken
place . . .

Is there any sickness that you are suffering from? . . . Physical, emotional, spiritual? . . . Speak to Jesus about it . . .
What does Jesus have to say? . . . Listen to his words to you,

"Do you want to get well?" Do you really mean what you say when you ask to be cured? . . . Are you ready to take all the consequences of a cure? . . . You have now arrived at a moment of grace . . . Do you have the faith that Jesus can cure you and that he means to cure you? . . . Do you have the trust that this will happen as a result of the faith of the whole group here? . . . Then listen to his mighty words as he pronounces the words of healing over you or lays his hands on you . . . What are you feeling? . . . Are you certain that those words you have heard are going to have an effect on you, in fact have already had their effect on you even though you may perceive nothing tangible at the moment? . . .

Spend a while now in quiet prayer in the company of Jesus . . .

Do not be discouraged if your first attempts at making this kind of contemplation meet with failure or do not satisfy you as much as you would wish. You will probably fare better in other attempts. When I conduct this particular contemplation in a group I invite the group members to share with us what they have experienced. Sometimes we even lay hands on one or others of them and pray over them in the name of Jesus.

This kind of contemplation offers theoretical difficulties to a number of people. They find it hard to plunge into an exercise that they know is so totally *unreal.* They have particular difficulty with a passage like the one I have chosen or with the infancy narratives. They do not realize the deep symbolic (which doesn't mean *unreal)* value of these contemplations. They are so enamored of the truth of history that they miss the truth of mystery. Truth for them is only historical, not mystical.

When Francis of Assisi lovingly took Jesus down from the Cross he surely knew that Jesus no longer died and was no longer hanging on the cross, that the crucifixion was a fact of past history. When Anthony of Padua held the Infant Jesus in his arms and regaled himself in his company he was surely aware, Doctor of the Church that he was, that Jesus is no longer an infant who can be held in one's arms. And yet these great saints and many others would practice this form of contemplation, and beneath these figures and fantasies that they lived out, something deep and mysterious was taking place within their hearts and they were becoming deeply united with God in Christ.

And so Teresa of Ávila would declare that her favorite form of meditation was to be present to Christ as he went through his agony in the garden. And Ignatius of Loyola will invite his exercitants to lovingly become a little servant and accompany Mary and Joseph on their journey to Bethlehem and serve them and converse with them and draw profit from his dealing with them in this way. He is not interested in geographical accuracy, so, even though he himself visited the Holy Places and could have given an accurate description of Bethlehem and Nazareth, he invites the exercitant to invent his own Bethlehem, his own Nazareth, the road to Bethlehem, the cave where Christ was born, etc. He was obviously not much concerned with historical accuracy in the sense in which we today understand it. He would certainly not have been deterred from this form of contemplation by form criticism and the findings of modern research into Scripture.

These contemplations must be undertaken with an attitude of faith, an attitude admirably depicted in a story that was a favorite with the saintly Hindu mystic Ramakrishna and his disciple Vivekananda. This is the story of a poor village boy who had to go to school to a neighboring village. He would go early in the morning when it was dark and return in the evening when it was getting dark. Now he had to cross a forest to get to school and he was frightened to go alone and asked his widowed mother to give him a servant for companion. Said his mother, "Son, we are too poor to afford a servant. Tell your Brother Krishna to accompany you to and from school. He is the Lord of the Jungle. He will surely come with you if you ask him to."

That is just what our little boy did. The next day he called out to his Brother Krishna, and when Krishna appeared and found

out what he wanted, he agreed to the boy's request. And so all
went well for a while.

Then came the village schoolmaster's birthday and all the children were expected to bring gifts for the master. The widow said
to her son, "We are too poor, son, to afford a gift for your master.
Ask your Brother Krishna to give you a gift for him." That is just
what Krishna did. He gave the boy a jug full of milk which the boy
proudly placed at the feet of the master, together with the many
other gifts that the other students had brought. The master just
ignored the gift, so, after a while, the child began to complain, as
children will, "Nobody is paying any attention to my gift . . . No
one seems to like my gift . . ." The master said to his servant,
"For heaven's sake, pour that milk into a basin and return the jug
to the boy, or we shall have no peace!"

The servant poured the milk into a vessel and was going to
return the jug when he noticed, to his surprise, that the jug was
full of milk again. Once again he emptied it. And once again it
automatically filled to the brim. When the master was told of this,
he called for the boy and asked him where he got that jug of milk.
"Brother Krishna gave it to me," was his answer. "Brother
Krishna? Who is he?" "He is the Lord of the Jungle," said the
little boy solemnly. "He accompanies me to and from school each
day." "Well," said the master, in open disbelief, "we'd like to see
this Krishna you speak of. Take us to him."

So the boy marched back to the jungle at the head of a little
group of people—the schoolmaster, the servant, and his fellow
students. He was delighted at the prospect of introducing everybody to his wonderful Brother Krishna. When they got to the
edge of the jungle where he met Krishna each day, he called out
to him, confident that he would come as he always did . . . But
there was no reply. He called out again. Then again. Then
louder. And louder. Still no reply . . . There was a lot of jeering
by now and a lot of fun among his fellow students. The boy was in
tears. What could have happened?

"Brother Krishna," he called out through his tears, "please

come. If you do not come they will say I am a liar. They won't believe me." There was a moment's silence, and then he heard the voice of Krishna clearly saying to him, "Son, I cannot come. The day your master has your purity of heart and your simple childlike faith I shall come."

The first thing that struck me when I heard that story was the Risen Lord's appearances. He appeared only to those who had faith in him. He could only be seen by those who believed in him. He says, "Believe, and then you will see." We say, "But then what proof will I have that my faith has not 'produced' the vision?" That is an irrelevant question to him. He is not interested in "proofs." Believe, then you will know. It is like saying to someone, "Love me and then you will see my beauty!"

This is the spirit in which we must embark upon these Ignatian contemplations. When we have launched out into them we will know that through the simple childlike use of our fantasy we have attained a truth far beyond fantasy, the truth of mystery, the truth of the mystics.

Exercise 23: Symbolic Fantasies

In a sense, all fantasy contemplations are symbolic. But the Ignatian fantasy contemplations are grounded on some element of history, which is not so with the ones I am going to propose to you now:

I want you to imagine you are sitting on top of a mountain that is overlooking a vast city. It is twilight, the sun has just set, and you notice the lights coming on in the great city . . . Watch them coming on until the whole city seems a lake of lights . . . You are sitting here all alone, gazing at this beautiful spectacle . . . What are you feeling? . . .

After a while you hear footsteps behind you and you know they are the footsteps of a holy man who lives in these parts, a hermit. He comes up to you and stands by your side. He looks at you gently and says just one sentence to you: "If you go down to the city tonight you will find God." Having said this, he turns around and walks away. No explanations. No time for questions . . .

You have a conviction that this man knows what he is talking about. What do you feel now? Do you feel like acting on his statement and going into the city? Or would you rather stay where you are?

Whatever your inclination, I want you now to go down to the city in search of God . . . What do you feel as you go down? . . .

You have now come to the outskirts of the city and you have to decide where to go to search for God and find him . . . Where do you decide to go? Please follow the dictates of your heart in choosing the place you go to. Don't be guided by what you think you "ought" to do or go to where you think you "ought" to go. Just go where your heart tells you to go . . .

What happens to you when you arrive at this place? . . . What do you find there? . . . What do you do there? . . . What happens to you? . . . Do you find God? . . . In what way? . . . Or are you disappointed? . . . What do you do then? . . . Do you choose to go somewhere else? . . . Where? . . . Or do you just stay where you are? . . .

Now I want you to change the fantasy. Whether you have found God or not, I want you to choose some symbol for God —anything you want that for you symbolizes God best—the face of a child, a star, a flower, a tranquil lake . . . What symbol do you choose? . . . Take your time choosing it . . .

Having chosen your symbol, stand reverently in front of it . . . What are you feeling as you gaze at this symbol? . . . Say something to it . . .

Now imagine that it speaks back to you . . . What does it say? . . .

I want you now to become this symbol . . . and, having

become the symbol, look at yourself standing out there reverently . . . What do you feel now as you see yourself from the
viewpoint and the attitude of this symbol? . . .

Now return to yourself standing there in front of the symbol
. . . Stay for a while in silent contemplation . . . Then say
good-bye to your symbol . . . Take a minute or two for this,
then open your eyes and end the exercise.

At the end of this exercise I generally invite the members of the
group to share with one another what they have experienced
during the fantasy. They frequently make startling discoveries
about themselves, about God, about their relationship with God.
Here is another symbolic fantasy:

A sculptor has been engaged to make a statue of you. The
statue is ready and you go to his studio to have a look at it
before it appears in public. He gives you the key to the room
where your statue is so that you can see it for yourself and take
all the time you want to examine it alone.

You open the door. The room is dark. There, in the middle
of the room is your statue, covered with a cloth . . . You walk
up to the statue and take the cloth off . . .

Then you step back and look at your statue. What is your first
impression? . . . Are you pleased or dissatisfied? . . . Notice all the details in your statue . . . How big it is . . . what
material it is made of . . . Walk around it . . . see it from
different angles . . . Look at it from far, then come closer and
look at the details . . . Touch the statue . . . notice whether
it is rough or smooth . . . cold or warm to the touch. What
parts of the statue do you like? . . . What parts of the statue
do you dislike? . . .

Say something to your statue . . . What does the statue
reply? . . . What do you say in return? . . . Keep on speaking as long as you or the statue have something to say . . .

Now become the statue . . . What does it feel like to be

your statue? . . . What kind of existence do you have as the statue? . . .

I want you to imagine now that, while you are your statue, Jesus walks into the room . . . How does he look at you? . . . What do you feel while he looks at you? . . . What does he say to you? . . . What do you reply? . . . Continue the dialogue as long as either Jesus or you have something to say . . .

After a while Jesus goes away . . . Now return to yourself and look at the statue again . . . Is there any change in the statue? . . . Is there any change in you or in your feelings? . . .

Now say good-bye to your statue . . . Take a minute or so to do this and then open your eyes.

Fantasies, like dreams, are useful tools for learning about yourself because you project your true self into your fantasies. That is why when you share your fantasy with someone or with a group you are probably revealing something more intimate about yourself than if you revealed deep secrets that you carefully guard from others.

Fantasies do not only give you insight into yourself. In some mysterious way they also change you! You sometimes come out of a fantasy feeling changed without quite knowing how or why the change has occurred. It is quite likely that in the two fantasies I have suggested here you find that your relationship with God has deepened, though you cannot explain why.

Do not be satisfied with doing these fantasies just once. To get the full profit from them you must do them again and again.

Then give vent to your creative instinct and invent your own symbolic fantasies.

Exercise 24:   Healing of Hurtful Memories

This is a variation of Exercise 19.

Return to some unpleasant event of the recent past, no matter how trifling. Relive the experience.

Now place yourself before Christ Crucified. Do not speak . . . Only look and contemplate . . . If you must communicate, do so without words . . .

Keep commuting between the unpleasant event and the scene of Jesus on the Cross for a few minutes . . . Then end the exercise.

Exercise 25:   The Value of Life

Imagine that you are going to the doctor to find out the results of tests that have been taken on you. The doctor is going to give them to you today. The tests could reveal some serious illness. Notice what you are feeling while you are on your way to the doctor's office . . .

You are now in his waiting room . . . Notice all the details of the room . . . the color of the walls, the prints on it . . . the furniture . . . the reviews and magazines there . . . Is there anyone else waiting for the doctor? . . . If there is, take a good look at the other person or persons in the room: their features, their clothes . . . Notice what you are feeling while you wait to be called into the office . . .

You are called in now . . . Take a look at the doctor's office . . . notice all the details, the furniture . . . Is the room bright or dim? . . . Take a good look at the doctor, his features, the way he is dressed . . . What kind of person is he? . . .

He begins to talk to you and you notice he seems to be hiding something from you . . . You tell him to speak to you quite openly . . . Then, with much compassion in his eyes, he tells you that the tests show that you have a disease that is incurable . . . You ask him how much longer you have to live . . . He says, "Two months of active life at the most . . . then a month or two in bed."

What is your response to this news? . . . What do you feel? . . . Stay for a while with those feelings . . . Now walk out of the doctor's office and into the street . . . Continue to stay with your feelings . . . Look at the street: is it crowded or empty? . . . Notice the weather: is the day a bright or a cloudy one? . . .

Where are you going? . . . Do you feel like talking with anyone? . . . With whom? . . .

You eventually get back to your community. (I am assuming that you are a religious priest or sister . . . Adaptations can easily be made for lay groups.) What do you say to your Superior? . . . Would you like the other members of the community to know? . . .

Your Superior asks you what you would like to do in the two months of active life you have, more or less indicating a readiness to let you choose any work you want . . . What do you choose to do? . . . How do you plan to spend those two months? . . .

You are at supper with the community now . . . at recreation . . . Do they know about you? . . . What are you feeling in their company? . . .

Go to your room now and write a letter to your Provincial Superior explaining the situation and asking to be eventually relieved of your work . . . What do you say in the letter? . . . Compose it in your mind right now . . .

It is late in the night now . . . Everyone in the community has gone to bed . . . You steal into the chapel where it is completely dark except for the soft glow of the sanctuary lamp

. . . You sit down and gaze at the tabernacle . . . Look at
Jesus for a while . . . What do you say to him? . . . What
does he say to you? . . . What are you feeling? . . .

The effects of this exercise are too varied to be enumerated
here. Most people enjoy returning to it again and again, never
ceasing to draw much fruit from it.

One of the things most people gain from this exercise is an
intense appreciation of and love for life . . . As a result, they
plunge more deeply into life, enjoying it, living it, using it more
fully . . . Many are surprised to find that they do not fear death
as much as they thought they would.

Too frequently it is only when we lose something that we
appreciate it and are grateful for it. No one is so grateful for sight
and so appreciative of it as the blind man. No one values health so
much as the sick man. But why do we have to wait till we lose
these things before we appreciate them and enjoy them?

Here are some other exercises for filling your life with gratitude and joyfulness:

Imagine that the doctor has examined your eyes and is going
to give you the result of his examination . . . Make the scene
as vivid as possible, noticing all the details of place and persons
as in the previous exercise . . .

The doctor now announces to you that your eyesight is fail-
ing, that there is nothing that medical science can do to save it,
and that, in all likelihood, you are going to be blind within
three or four months . . . What are your feelings? . . .

You are now aware that you have only three or four months
to imprint on your memory sights that you will never see again
. . . What do you especially want to see before you go blind?
. . . Notice how you look at things, now that you know you are
soon going to be blind forever . . .

Imagine now that you have, indeed, become blind . . .
What kind of existence do you lead as a blind person? . . .
Take time out to get into all your dispositions and feelings

. . . In fantasy go through your whole day as a blind person, from the moment you rise and wash in the morning till the moment you go to bed at night . . . Take your meals, "read" books, talk to people, go for a walk . . . as a blind person . . .

Now open your eyes and realize that you can see . . . What do you feel? . . . What do you say to God? . . .

The best things in life are free—things like sight and health and love and freedom and life itself. The pity is that we do not really enjoy them. We are too worried about the fact that we do not have enough of things that are very secondary: things like money and fine clothes and fame among men. I remember returning home on a plane once and being irritated by the fact that the plane was late. Then, having arrived over the airport, the plane began to circle for nearly half an hour—thereby adding to our delay— because of what was discreetly termed "technical difficulties" . . . It was a half hour full of suspense and anxiety. You can imagine the relief we felt when we finally landed. What happened to our irritation at being late? Not a trace of it was left. We were overjoyed that we were well and safe—arriving late was just a silly trifle. And yet, it took the possibility of a serious accident to make us appreciate this.

I once read the account of a Nazi prisoner who wrote home to his family in great delight to say he had been shifted from a cell that consisted of only four bare walls to another where there was an opening high up in one wall through which he could get a glimpse of the blue sky in the morning and a few stars at night. This, to him, was an immense treasure. After reading that letter, I looked out of my window at the whole expanse of the sky . . . I was a million times richer than that poor prisoner but did not get a fraction of the joy from my riches that he got from his little store. In fact, I was deriving no joy from it at all!

Think of what life is like for a prisoner, for an inmate of a concentration camp . . . and when you have really got into his life and his feelings, take a bus ride round the city, enjoying all the sights and relishing your freedom!

Here is one more exercise of this type. You can then invent others of a similar nature so that your heart will be brimming over with gratitude to God for all the lovely things you possess.

Imagine you are in a hospital and paralyzed . . . It might help for you to lie on the floor if you are in a group, or on your bed if you are alone while you do this exercise. Imagine that you cannot move a single limb of your body from your neck down . . .

In fantasy go through your whole day as a paralyzed person . . . What do you do all day? . . . What do you think? . . . What do you feel? . . . How do you keep yourself occupied? . . .

In this state, be aware that you still have your sight . . . Be grateful for that . . . Then become aware that you have your sense of hearing . . . Be grateful for that too . . . Then become aware that you can still think lucidly . . . that you can speak and express yourself . . . that you have the sense of taste, which brings you pleasure . . . Be grateful for each one of these gifts of God . . . Realize how rich you are in spite of your paralysis! . . .

Now imagine that after a while you begin to respond to treatment and it is possible for you to move your neck. Painfully at first, then with greater ease, you can turn your head from one side to another . . . A much wider area of vision is offered you. You can now look from one end of the ward to the other without having to have your whole body moved by someone else . . . Notice how grateful you feel for this too . . .

Now come back to your present existence and realize that you are not paralyzed. Move your fingers gently and realize there is life and movement in them. Wriggle your toes . . . Move your arms and legs . . . Say a prayer of thanksgiving to God over each one of these limbs . . .

The day you can be grateful for every single trifle in your life, for the moving train, for the water that runs down a tap when you open it, for the light that comes on when you press a switch, for clean sheets on your bed . . . your heart will be filled with a deep contentment and with almost continual joy. The secret of being always joyful is to be always grateful.

Try this exercise in the area of human relations: When you resent a friend or someone in your family, spend some time imagining that he is much worse than you think he is now, that he has many more defects than the ones you see in him now . . . Then notice all the good things he has . . . You will probably become more appreciative of him, you will become more grateful for him, and you will find it much, much easier to *forgive* him.

Exercise 26:   Seeing Life in Perspective

This is a variation of the previous exercise on the value of life:

In continuation of the previous exercise, I want you now to imagine that, after the two months of active life the doctor said you would have, you are now bedridden . . . Where are you? . . . Take a good look at your surroundings . . . What kind of life are you leading now? . . . How do you spend your day? . . .

Imagine it is evening now and you have been left alone . . . You are not sure how many more days of life you have . . . How do you feel about the fact that you do not have much longer to live? . . . that you are no longer able to be active? . . .

In the solitude that is now yours I want you to look back on your life . . . Recall some of the happy moments of your life . . .

Recall some of the sad moments . . . What do you feel now

as you look back on the events that caused you pain and distress? . . .

Recall some of the important decisions that you made, decisions that affected your life or the lives of others. Do you regret them or rejoice that you made them? . . . Are there any decisions you think you ought to have made and did not? . . .

Spend some ten minutes now remembering some of the significant people in your life . . . What faces come most readily to your mind? . . . What are your feelings as you think of each of these persons?

If you were given the chance to live life again, would you accept it? . . . Would you place any conditions to accepting it? . . .

If you had to give just one piece of advice to your friends or say just one sentence to them in farewell, what would you say?

After a while, turn to Christ. Imagine him standing at your bedside and speak to him . . .

And yet another exercise connected with your death:

Jesus knew when he was going to die and he planned the last hours of his life carefully. He chose to spend them with his friends at a final meal and then with his Father in prayer before his arrest.

If you had the opportunity to plan the last few hours of your life, how would you choose to spend them? Would you want to be alone or with others? If you want others near you, whom do you want?

At his last supper Jesus made a final prayer to his Father. What is the last prayer you would want to make to God?

One of the great fruits of these fantasies on death is to give us not only a fresh appreciation for life but also a sense of urgency. An oriental writer compares death to a hunter crouched behind bushes taking aim at a duck that swims placidly on the lake, totally unaware of the danger it is in. The aim of these fantasies is not to make you feel fear but to help you avoid wastage in your life.

Exercise 27: Saying Good-bye to Your Body

Imagine now that you have said your final farewells to everyone before you die and you have just about an hour or two of life left. You have reserved this time for yourself and for God . . .

So begin by speaking to yourself. Talk to each of the limbs of your body: your hands, your feet, your heart, your brain, your lungs . . . Say a final farewell to each of them . . . You may be taking explicit notice of them for the very first time in your life—now that you are about to die!

Love each one of your limbs. Take your right hand, for instance . . . Thank it for all the service it has given you . . . Tell it how precious it is to you . . . how much you love it . . . Give it all your love and gratitude now that it is going to turn into dust very soon . . . Do this in turn for each of the limbs and organs of your body, then for your body as a whole, with its special form and appearance and color and height and features.

Now imagine that you see Jesus near you. Listen to him thank each of the members of your body for the service it has given you in life . . . See him fill the whole of your body with his love and gratitude . . .

Listen to him speak to you now . . .

This exercise is a very valuable one for attaining that healthy love of oneself and acceptance of oneself without which it is so hard to fully give our hearts to God and to others.

Exercise 28:   Your Funeral

This exercise is meant to reinforce the good effect of the previous one, to give you a further love and appreciation for yourself.

Imagine you see your body in its coffin laid out in a church for the funeral rites . . . Take a good look at your body, especially at the expression on your face . . .

Now look at all the people who have come to your funeral . . . Go slowly from one pew to another looking at the faces of these people . . . Stop before each person and see what he is thinking and what he is feeling . . .

Now listen to the sermon that is being preached. Who is the preacher? . . . What is he saying about you? . . .

Can you accept all the good things he is saying about you? . . . If you cannot, notice what resistances there are in you to accepting what the preacher is saying . . . Which of the good things he says about you are you willing to accept? How do you feel when you hear him speak? . . .

Look again at the faces of your friends who have come to attend your funeral . . . Imagine all the good things they will be saying about you when they return home from your funeral . . . What do you feel now? . . .

Is there something you would like to say to each of them before they go home? . . . Some final farewell in response to all they are thinking and feeling about you, a response which, alas, they will never hear now? . . . Say it, all the same, and see what this does to you . . .

Imagine that the funeral rites are over now. You stand in imagination above the grave in which your body lies, watching your friends leave the cemetery. What are your feelings now? . . . As you stand here now, look back on your life and your experiences . . . Was it all worthwhile? . . .

Now become aware of your existence here in the room and realize that you are still alive and still have some time at your disposal . . . Think of these same friends now from your present point of view. Do you see them differently as a result of this exercise? Think of yourself now . . . Do you see yourself differently or feel differently about yourself as a result of this exercise? . . .

Exercise 29:   Fantasy on the Corpse

I have borrowed this exercise from the Buddhist series of *reality meditations*. If it causes you repugnance at first sight and you feel disinclined to attempt it, I would have you know that the purpose of this meditation is to offer you the gift of peace and joy and help you to live life in greater depth. This has been the experience of many people. It may be yours too.

For this exercise I want you to imagine as vividly as you can your own corpse and to watch it in fantasy as it goes through the nine stages of decomposition. Spend about a minute or so on each stage.

These are the nine stages: 1. The corpse is cold and rigid.   2. It is turning blue.   3. Cracks appear in the flesh.   4. Decomposition sets in in some parts.   5. The whole body is in full decomposition.   6. The skeleton now appears with some flesh adhering to it in some places.   7. Now you have only the skeleton with no flesh on it at all.   8. Now all that exists is a heap of bones.   9. The bones are all reduced now to a handful of dust.

Exercise 30: Consciousness of the Past

To do this exercise, you have to think of your whole day as a film. Let us suppose you are doing this exercise at night. You unwind the film of the day, going backward, one scene at a time, until you return to the first scene of the morning, your first waking moment.

For instance, what is the last thing you did before starting this exercise? You walked into this room and took your seat and composed yourself for prayer. That will be the first scene you will contemplate. What happened before that? You walked to this room. That will be your second scene. And before that? You stopped to chat with a friend on the way. That will be your third scene . . .

Take one scene, one unit of actions, at a time and observe everything you are doing, thinking, feeling in the scene. Do not relive the scene. Unlike the other fantasy exercises I gave you earlier, you are not to participate in these events as if they were taking place again, but to merely observe them from the outside. Look at them in a detached manner, as a neutral observer would.

Take some time first to quieten yourself, because this exercise demands a great quietness inside you . . . Do one of the awareness exercises to quieten your mind and come to the present moment . . .

Now begin to unroll the *film*, going back over each of the events of the day . . . Take your time and see each of the events in some detail . . . Take a look especially at the principal actor, yourself . . . Notice how he acts, what he is thinking, how he is feeling . . .

It is very important that while you observe these events you adopt a neutral attitude, that is, that you neither condemn nor approve of what you are observing . . . Just observe. Do not judge. Do not evaluate . . .

If you are distracted in the course of this exercise see if you can trace the distraction back to its source as soon as you become aware that you are distracted. In other words, suppose you find yourself thinking of your next meal. Ask yourself how you came to this point. What was the thought that preceded this thought about your next meal? And the thought before that? And before that? . . . Till you come to the point where you branched off from your task of unrolling the film.

Keep at this exercise till you get to the first moment of the day, your first waking moment . . .

This is an extremely difficult exercise to perform successfully. It requires an intense degree of recollectedness and a great mastery of the art of concentration. This type of concentration comes only to those who are deeply at peace within themselves and have managed to get that peace to pervade their minds and their other faculties. So do not be discouraged if your first attempts meet with considerable failure. The mere attempt to unroll that film will do you a lot of good and you will probably get a good deal of profit from observing no more than one or two scenes or events. The oriental masters who propose this exercise claim that those who have mastered it (and have, accordingly, mastered their minds sufficiently to be able to perform it successfully) are able to recollect with perfect clarity not only every single event of the past day, but every event of the past week and month and year and years . . .

If you find that the attempt to trace distractions back to their source is itself a great distraction, then drop the attempt altogether. The moment you realize you are distracted return to the last scene that you were contemplating before you were distracted. To attempt to retrace the distractions to their source might be undertaking too many difficult tasks at once.

The injunction about neither approving nor condemning is

based on the teaching of some oriental masters that approval and condemnation are not needed to reform your life and actions. The use of will power to make resolutions and the self-punishment involved in condemnation may provoke a resistance within you and you will needlessly be caught up in an inner conflict, the action producing an equal and opposite reaction.

Self-awareness avoids this danger. The postulate is that awareness alone will heal, without the need for judgments and resolutions. Mere awareness will cause to die whatever is unhealthy and will cause to grow whatever is good and holy. It is like the sun that gives life to plants and destroys germs. There is no need to use your spiritual or psychological muscles to achieve this. Only become calm and collected and peaceful—and be aware. Be as fully conscious as possible. This, of course, is a postulate. When you have become familiar with the power of self-awareness, it will cease to be a postulate and become a matter of personal experience.

You can now go one step further in your exercise.

Unroll that film once again and observe each of the events of the day, one at a time . . .

When you have gone through a series of events, choose one of them, the one you consider the most significant, and observe it in greater detail . . .

Every gesture, every word, every feeling, every thought, every reaction says something about *you*. Notice what they are saying . . .

Do not analyze. Only *look* . . .

And one final step:

Repeat the previous exercise, going over one of the events in greater detail . . .

Christ was in that event. Where was he? Can you observe him acting in it? How does he act? . . .

Exercise 31:   Awareness of the Future

This is a variation of the previous exercise, only the subject matter of this one is the events of the future, not the past, and this exercise is more appropriate for the morning, while the previous one is more appropriate for the night.

Starting from this present moment, go over the events of the day ahead of you, events that are likely to happen . . . You cannot be quite sure, of course, but take those events that are likely to occur with a fair amount of probability: an interview with someone, your meals, your prayer time, your journey to and from work . . .

Observe each of these events as they are likely to happen . . . Do not attempt to correct them or improve on them . . . Only look. Only observe . . .

The next step:

Now go over those events again and see yourself behaving (thinking, feeling, reacting) the way you would like to behave . . . No resolutions, please! Just *SEE* yourself in imagination behaving as you would like to behave . . .

Then see those events as you would like them to be . . .

The final step:

Return to each of those events . . . Find Christ and his action in each of them . . .

Return to the present moment and end the exercise with a prayer to Christ, who is present to you now . . .

Another variation:

Reflect for a moment that you are a manifestation of God to the world. God appears to everyone you meet today in your form and figure . . .

Now go over those future events and see this manifestation of God in action . . . No condemnations and judgments! And, above all, no resolutions! Only look. Only see those events as they are likely to occur. Or as you would like them to occur . . .

Exercise 32:   Awareness of Persons

This is a simple variation of the previous two exercises. It is based on the knowledge that Jesus Christ, the Risen Lord, makes his appearance in our lives in a form in which we do not at first recognize him. This was the experience of the Apostles after the resurrection. They would first see him as a stranger (on the road to Emmaus, on the shore of Lake Tiberias, at the tomb where he appeared to Mary of Magdala as the gardener) and only later would they recognize him for what he was.

This exercise will help you to recognize the Risen Lord in the face of each of the persons you are going to meet today.

Repeat the previous exercise, going over some of the events that are likely to take place today . . .

Now dwell especially on each of the persons who are likely to enter into your daily routine . . . Make the reflection that each of them is the Risen Lord himself appearing to you in disguise . . .

Recognize the Lord in each of them . . . Love him, adore him, serve him . . . even allowing yourself forms of adoration and service and love in your fantasy which you would not allow yourself to indulge in in reality . . .

At the end of the exercise come to the present moment . . . Become aware of the presence of Jesus with you in this room . . . Adore him. Speak to him . . .

This exercise is the last of our fantasy exercises. Fantasy is a very valuable element in our prayer life, as it is in any healthy emotional life. If it is used judiciously, namely, as a means to deepen our recollection and our inner silence rather than as a means of pleasant entertainment, our prayer life will be greatly enriched, as you will have discovered from using some of these exercises.

Saint Teresa of Ávila, who scaled the heights of mystical union with God, was a great advocate of the use of fantasy in prayer. She had a very distracted mind and couldn't find any inner silence, even for a few minutes. Her way of praying, she said, was enclosing herself within herself, but she couldn't do this without simultaneously enclosing a thousand vanities.

She lived to be grateful for the fact that her mind was such a scattered one, because she was forced to take her prayer out of the realm of thought and into the realm of affection and fantasy. She recommends the use of images. Imagine you see Jesus in his agony in the garden and console him there. Imagine your heart to be a lovely garden and Christ walks there among the flowers. Imagine your soul is a beautiful palace with crystalline walls and God is a brilliant diamond at the very heart of this palace. Imagine your soul is a paradise, a heaven where you will be flooded with delights. Imagine you are a sponge soaked through and through, not with water, but with the presence of God. See God as a fountain at the very center of your being. Or as a brilliant sun giving light to every part of your being, sending its rays out from the center of your heart.

Each one of those images would serve as a whole fantasy contemplation in itself. Together with the use of fantasy, Teresa recommends the use of the heart in prayer. And it is to this form of prayer that we now address ourselves in the following exercises.

DEVOTION

Exercise 33: The "Benedictine" Method

This is a form of prayer that was widely used for centuries in the Church and has been attributed to Saint Benedict, who popularized it and refined its use. It has traditionally been divided into three parts: *lectio* (or sacred reading), *meditatio* (meditation), and *oratio* (prayer).

Here is one way of practicing this form of prayer:

Start by quietening yourself in the presence of God . . . Then take up a book for sacred reading, *lectio*, and begin reading until you alight upon a word, a phrase, a sentence that appeals to you, that attracts you . . . When you get to such a sentence, stop the *lectio*. The first part of the exercise is now over and the second part, the meditation, must begin.

A word about the book you choose for reading. Almost any book will do provided it is likely to foster unction and prayer rather than speculation. The ideal book for this is the Bible. *The Imitation of Christ* of Thomas à Kempis is another book that lends itself to this form of prayer. So do the writings of the Fathers, or any other devotional book, such as Brother Lawrence's *The Practice of the Presence of God.*

It is important that you do not take a passage for your reading that you are not familiar with, that is likely to spur you on to read more and more. The purpose of this reading is to awaken your heart to prayer, not to stimulate your mind to curiosity. Curiosity can be either a priceless asset to a creative mind or a subtle form of laziness. It becomes a form of laziness when it leads us away from the seemingly dull task we have at hand.

Let us suppose now that you have taken for your *lectio* a passage from the New Testament or from the Psalms, two parts of the Bible that lend themselves ideally to this kind of prayer. I shall take, as a sample, one of my favorite passages, John 7:37–38. You begin to read:

> The last day of the feast was the most important. On that day Jesus stood up and said in a loud voice: "If any man is thirsty, let him come to me and drink. He who believes in me, streams of living water will pour out from his heart . . ."

And let us suppose that you are gripped, as I always am, by those words, *"If any man is thirsty, let him come to me and drink."* Then the lectio stops and the *meditatio* begins.

The *meditatio* is done, not with one's mind, but with one's mouth. *"The mouth of the just man shall meditate wisdom,"* we are told in the Bible. When the psalmist tells us how he loves to meditate on the law of God, how he finds it sweeter to his palate than honey from the honeycomb, how he meditates on this law of God ceaselessly, day and night, is he talking about meditation merely as an intellectual exercise, a reflection of what is stated in God's law? I like to think that he is also talking about the constant recitation of God's law—so he meditates as much with his mouth as with his head. This is what you must now do with this sentence:

> Repeat this sentence again and again. You may do this mentally; there is no need to pronounce the words with your mouth or to say them aloud. What is important, however, is that you keep repeating these words (even if you do so mentally) and reduce your reflection on their meaning to the barest minimum. In fact, it is better not to reflect on them at all. You know what they mean. Now, through repetition of them, allow them to sink into your heart and mind, to become part of you . . .
> *If any man is thirsty, let him come to me and drink . . . If any man is thirsty, let him come to me and drink . . . If any man is thirsty . . .*
> As you do this, you will savor and relish the words you are repeating . . . It is likely that you will instinctively shorten the

sentence, dwelling now on one set of words rather than on another. *If any man is thirsty . . . any man . . . any man . . . any man . . .*

Once you have done this for a while, you will have relished the words sufficiently. You will feel saturated with them, touched by the unction they give. Now is the time to stop the meditation and start the prayer, the *oratio*.

How is the oratio made? Either by speaking spontaneously to the Lord in whose presence you are, or by maintaining a loving silence in his presence, filled as you are with the grace, the unction, the attitude that these words have induced in you. Thus, you might proceed somewhat in this fashion:

"*Any man . . . any man . . . any man . . .* Do you really mean that, Lord? Are you ready to give any man living water to drink? Is it true that we need no qualification except that of being a man? That it does not matter if I am a sinner or a saint, if I love you or I don't, if I have been faithful to you in the past or not? That it is enough that I am just a thirsty man—and that I come to you? . . ."

Or you might say something like this: "*Thirsty, thirsty . . . thirsty . . . come to me . . . come to me . . . come to me . . .* I am thirsty, Lord, so here I come to you . . . But I am coming with a good deal of diffidence . . . I have come to you so often in the past and you have not slaked my thirst . . . What is this mysterious living water that you speak of? Is there some block in me that prevents my seeing it . . . my tasting it? . . ."

Pray spontaneously in this fashion, or just stay in loving silence before the Lord as I suggested above, as long as you can do so without being distracted. When you notice you are finding it hard to maintain the *oratio* without distraction, pick up your book and start the *lectio* again. Go ahead in the passage you have chosen until you alight upon another sentence that appeals to you . . .

Saint Benedict says, "*Oratio sit brevis et pura.*" Let prayer be brief *and pure.* He is not speaking here of the time we give to meditation and prayer in general. He is speaking of the third part of this method of prayer, the *oratio,* which should be held on to as long as it is *pure,* that is, distractionless. When distractions begin to come in, it is time to move on to the *lectio.* This *oratio* will often have to be brief for beginners, who are not accustomed to being long without distractions.

This is an excellent form of prayer to recommend to those whom you wish to initiate into the art of praying with the heart rather than with the head. It offers the head some participation in prayer and thus keeps it from being distracted. At the same time it gently takes the prayer away from discourse and reflection into simplicity and affectivity.

You will find in the psalms a gold mine for the practice of this form of prayer. Who can resist the force of phrases like these that are found lavishly scattered all over the Book of Psalms?

My body pines for you
like dry, weary land without water.
On you I muse all through the night. *(Psalm 63)*

One thing I long for—to live in the house of the Lord.
It is your face, O Lord, that I seek. *(Psalm 27)*

My soul is longing for the Lord
more than watchmen for daybreak. *(Psalm 130)*

In God alone is my soul at rest;
my help comes from him. *(Psalm 62)*

Some trust in chariots or horses,
but we in the name of the Lord. *(Psalm 20)*

In my anguish I cried for help.
God is the rock where I take refuge.
You, O God, are the lamp of my darkness.
With you I can break any barrier.
God is indeed a shield
to all who take refuge in him. *(Psalm 18)*

O that I had wings like a dove
to fly away and be at rest!
Entrust your cares to the Lord
and he will support you. *(Psalm 55)*
Do not deprive me of your holy spirit.
Give me again the joy of your help. *(Psalm 51)*

There is a form of practicing this method of prayer in a group. The leader leads the group through an awareness exercise as a help to each member to deepen the silence within . . . Or he invites the group to deepen its silence through any means that each member finds most useful . . . After a number of minutes of silence, the group leader chants a phrase from the Scriptures in a loud, clear voice, then lapses into silence, allowing time for the members to let the words sink into their hearts . . . The deeper the silence in your heart, the more powerful will be the impact of the words. If you find the words distracting, do not pay attention to them; merely incorporate the sound of the words into your world of awareness.

Another variation is to have the group chant the words after the leader and to chant each sentence two or three times. Be careful to allow a lot of time for silence, both for the words to sink in and for the creation of an atmosphere that is receptive of the next words that will be chanted.

Exercise 34: Vocal Prayer

Most people are familiar with the distinction between vocal prayer and mental prayer. Vocal prayer is popularly considered to be prayer that is recited. Mental prayer is generally considered to be prayer that is made with one's mind and heart. Vocal prayer is also frequently thought of as more apt for beginners in the spiritual life, for people who are not developed enough mentally to go in for serious reflection, and so it is thought of as a form of prayer that is decidedly inferior to mental prayer.

The popular opinion in this matter is quite erroneous. It was only toward the Middle Ages that this clear-cut distinction between vocal and mental prayer was made in the Church. Before that, people could hardly conceive of a person's praying without using words. To say to men like Saint Augustine or Saint Ambrose or Saint John Chrysostom what we say to our spiritual aspirants today, *"Don't say prayers; pray,"* would be to say something they just would not have understood. They would have wondered how one could pray without saying prayers.

They were perfectly aware of those periods of prayer that come upon a contemplative when, in the words of Saint Teresa of Ávila, God takes the words out of your mouth, so that even if you want to speak you will not be able to, and when a total silence descends on you that makes all words and thoughts superfluous. But they, and most of the great masters in the art of prayer, were of the opinion that praying with words is much more likely to bring you to that state than praying with *thoughts*.

One such master was Saint John Climacus, who initiated people into the art of prayer through a method that is so obvious that it is largely ignored. Here is his method in substance:

Become aware of God, in whose presence you are while you pray . . . Then take a formula of prayer and recite it with perfect attention both to the words you are saying and to the Person to whom you are saying them.

Let us suppose you choose the Lord's Prayer. Begin to recite it from start to finish with perfect attention: *"Our Father in heaven, Holy be your name, Your kingdom come, Your will be done on earth as it is in heaven . . . . "* meaning each word that you recite.

If at any point you are distracted, return to the word or phrase where you got distracted and repeat it, if necessary again and again, until you can say it with perfect attention.

When you have gone through the whole formula with perfect

attention, go over it again and again. Or move on to some other prayer formula.

This was all the *method* that many of the saints used in their prayer. And they made considerable progress in the art of prayer and contemplation on the basis of this alone. Saint Teresa of Ávila tells of a simple lay sister who begged her to teach her *contemplation*. Teresa asked her how she prayed and found that all she did was recite very devoutly the Our Father and Hail Mary five times in honor of the five wounds of the Saviour. Teresa also discovered that on the basis of these vocal prayers alone, and nothing else, this good lay sister had reached the heights of contemplation and needed no lessons at all in being a contemplative.

Here is another form of practicing vocal prayer. Take a prayer formula or a psalm. Recite it through once and notice the words that you can say most easily and the words that come to you with the greatest difficulty.

Here is Psalm 23:

The Lord is my shepherd;
there is nothing I shall want.
Fresh and green are the pastures
Where he gives me repose.
Near restful waters he leads me,
to revive my drooping spirit.

He guides me along the right path;
he is true to his name.
If I should walk in the valley of darkness
no evil would I fear.
You are there with your crook and your staff;
with these you give me comfort.

You have prepared a banquet for me
in the sight of my foes.
My head you have anointed with oil;
my cup is overflowing.

Surely goodness and kindness shall follow me
all the days of my life.
In the Lord's own house shall I dwell,
for ever and ever.

Choose the one line in that psalm that appeals to you the most—the one that comes most easily to you—your favorite line in the whole psalm. Recite it again and again . . . Feed your hungry spirit on it . . . You may do the same with one or two other lines that particularly appeal to you.

Now choose the line that you have the greatest difficulty saying . . . Recite it again and again and notice what you feel . . . what happens to you when you recite it . . . what it says to you about yourself or about your dealings with God . . . Then pray spontaneously to God about this.

As you move along the pathways of prayer, you will make sure, if you are wise, to take provisions with you—a small stock of your favorite vocal prayers and hymns and psalms that you can always fall back on in time of need.

People sometimes complain that these prayers are *impersonal* because they are ready-made formulas, but this is not accurate. No two people recite the Lord's Prayer in quite the same way. When you recite the words of the Lord's Prayer, those words go down into your heart and mind. They shape you, they take on the coloring that you give them, and then they ascend to God with the distinctive, personal stamp that you have given them. So those formulas do not have to be impersonal at all.

Exercise 35:   The Jesus Prayer

The ceaseless repetition of the name of Jesus is a form of prayer very dear to Greek and Russian Orthodox Christians, who find in this form of prayer the firm foundation of their prayer life and their spiritual life in general. I recommend that you read the book

The Way of a Pilgrim to get some idea of the value of this prayer and the way it is practiced.

This is a form of prayer that has been highly developed among Hindus in India over a period of thousands of years. It is called the Remembrance of the Name. Mahatma Gandhi, who was a zealous advocate of this form of prayer, claimed that it brought with it the most extraordinary benefits for spirit and mind and body. He claimed to have overcome all his fears, even as a child, simply through the ceaseless repetition of God's name. He said there was more power in its recitation than in the atom bomb. He even went to the extent of claiming that he would not die of any sickness, that if he were to die of some sickness people could consider him a hypocrite! According to him, reciting God's name with faith would cure a man of any disease whatsoever. Only he must recite the Name with all his heart and soul and mind during the time of prayer.

Outside the time of prayer even a mechanical recitation of the Name will do. Through this seemingly mechanical recitation the Name gets into one's bloodstream, as it were, into the very depths of one's unconscious and of one's being—and, very subtly but surely, one's heart and life are transformed.

In this and in some of the following exercises I propose some ways of reciting the Name in time of prayer. I limit myself mostly to the Name of Jesus. All the masters assert that any name of God will do to attain the benefits that this prayer brings with it. Some of you may want to take for your *mantra* the name of God that the Spirit cries out within our hearts: *Abba, Father.*

Begin your prayer by asking for the help of the Holy Spirit. It is only in the power of the Spirit that we can worthily pronounce the name of Jesus . . .

Then imagine Jesus before you. In what form do you like best to imagine him? As the Infant, as the Crucified Christ, as the Risen Lord . . . ?

Where do you imagine him to be? Standing before you?

Some are greatly helped to imagine the Lord as being en-shrined within their hearts . . . or within their heads. Some of the Hindu masters recommend the center of the forehead, somewhere between the eyes . . . Choose the place that you find most devotional in which to imagine you see him . . .

Now pronounce the name of Jesus each time you breathe in or each time you breathe out . . . Or you may pronounce the first syllable of his name as you breathe in and the second syllable as you breathe out. If you find this too frequent, then pronounce the name after every three or four breaths. It is important that you do this gently, relaxed, and peacefully . . .

If you are in the presence of others, you will have to recite the name mentally. If you are alone, you may pronounce it vocally, in a soft voice . . .

If, after a while, you tire of pronouncing the Name, rest for a while, then take up the recitation again, somewhat as a bird does when it flaps its wings for a while and then glides for a while, then flaps its wings again . . .

Notice what you feel when you pronounce his name . . .

After a while, pronounce his name with different sentiments and attitudes. First pronounce it with desire. Without saying the words *"Lord, I desire you,"* convey this sentiment to him through the way you recite his name . . .

Do this for some time, then take up another attitude. One of trust. Through your recitation of his name say to him, *"Lord, I trust you."* Go on, after some time, to other sentiments, to adoration and love and repentance and praise and gratitude and surrender . . .

Now imagine you hear him pronounce your name . . . as he pronounced Mary of Magdala's name on the morning of the resurrection . . . No one will ever pronounce your name in quite the way that Jesus does . . . With what sentiments does he pronounce your name? What do you feel when you hear him pronounce your name?

Among the Orthodox it is customary to recite the name of Jesus within the *Jesus Prayer formula.* The formula is *"Lord Jesus Christ, have mercy on me."* Here is a method for using this formula:

After a time spent in quietening yourself, become aware of the presence of the Risen Lord . . . Imagine him standing before you . . .

Now concentrate on your breathing for a while, becoming aware of the air as it comes into you and goes out . . .

When you breathe in, say the first part of the formula, *Lord Jesus Christ,* and, as you do so, imagine you are breathing into yourself the love and grace and presence of the Lord Jesus . . . Imagine you are breathing into yourself all the loveliness of his being.

Then hold your breath for a brief moment in your lungs, and as you do this, imagine you are holding in yourself what you have breathed in, that your whole being is suffused with his presence and his grace . . .

As you breathe out, say the second part of the formula, *Have mercy on me* . . . As you do this, imagine you are breathing out of yourself all your impurities, all the obstacles you are putting in the way of his grace . . .

The words *Have mercy on me* do not mean just *Pardon my sins.* Mercy, as the Orthodox use the word, means much more: it means grace and loving-kindness. So when you are asking for mercy, you are asking for Christ's graciousness and loving-kindness and for the anointing of his Spirit.

Exercise 36:   The Thousand Names of God

This exercise is an adaptation from the Hindu practice of reciting the thousand names of God. Devout Hindus may take the trouble to memorize the thousand names of God in Sanskrit—each name is full of meaning and reveals some aspect of the divinity—and to recite these names lovingly in time of prayer.

I propose that you now invent a thousand names for Jesus. Imitate the psalmist, who is not satisfied with the usual names of God like Lord, Saviour, King, but, with the creativity that comes from a heart full of love, invents fresh names for God. *You are my rock*, he will say, *my shield, my fortress, my delight, my song* . . .

So you too, in this exercise, give vent to your creativity and invent names for Jesus: *Jesus, my joy . . . Jesus, my strength . . . Jesus, my love . . . Jesus, my delight . . . Jesus, my peace . . .*

Each time you breathe out, recite one of these names of Jesus . . . If one name or other appeals to you particularly, repeat it again and again . . . Or recite it once and then rest lovingly in it for a while, saying nothing . . . and then take up another name . . . rest in it . . . then move on to another . . .

Now comes a part of the exercise that you may find very moving:

Imagine you hear Jesus inventing names for you! What names does he invent for you? . . . What do you feel when you hear him call you by these names? . . .

People frequently turn away from listening to the loving words that God is saying to them. It is more than they can take. It is too good to be true. So they either hear Jesus say negative things to them like, *Sinner* . . . etc., or they go blank and hear him say nothing. They have still to discover the God of the New Testament, whose love for them is unconditional and infinite. They have still to allow themselves to feel his love. This exercise is well suited to that purpose.

Go one step further now and imagine you hear Jesus inventing for you exactly the same names that you invented for him—all the names, except those that directly express divinity

. . . Do not be frightened . . . expose yourself to the intensity of his love!

You may have misgivings, as many do, about imagining you hear Christ say things to you. In some of the fantasy exercises, I recommended that you talk to Christ and imagine him talking to you. You may ask, "How am I to know whether it is really Christ who is saying these words to me or whether I am just inventing them? Is it Christ who is talking to me or is it I who am talking to myself through this image of Christ that I have conjured up?"

The answer to that question is that, in all likelihood, it is you who are talking to yourself through this image of Christ that your fantasy has produced. However, beneath the surface of this dialogue that you have with this imaginary Christ, the Lord will begin to work in your heart. It won't be long before you will experience this imaginary Christ saying something to you, and the effect of his words will be such (in the way of consolation, of light and inspiration, of a fresh infusion of joy and strength) that you will know in your heart that those words either came directly from the Lord or were your own invention and were used by the Lord to communicate to you what he wanted.

For the purpose of this exercise, however, you do not have to worry about the objection that the words you hear from the lips of Christ may be an invention of your own. The love of Jesus for you is so great that no words you invent and put in his lips to express it will ever prove adequate!

Exercise 37: See Him Looking at You

Here is another exercise for allowing yourself to experience the love of Christ for you, a favorite exercise of Saint Teresa of Ávila. It is one of those fundamental exercises that she recommended to everybody.

Imagine you see Jesus standing before you . . . He is looking at you . . . Notice him looking at you . . .

That is all! Teresa puts it in a very brief formula: *"Mira que te
mira."* Notice that he is looking at you.

She adds two very important adverbs, however. *Notice that he is
looking at you,* she says, *lovingly and humbly.* Take particular care to
feel both attitudes in Christ as he looks at you: see him look at you
with love; see him look at you with humility.

Both of these attitudes can cause difficulty. Many find it hard to
imagine Jesus looking at them lovingly—their image of Jesus is
the image of someone who is harsh and demanding, someone
who, even if he loves them, loves them only if they are good. The
second attitude they find even more difficult to accept: that Jesus
should look at them humbly . . . Impossible! Once again, they
have not understood the Jesus of the New Testament. They have
never taken seriously the fact that Jesus has become their servant
and slave, the one who washes their feet, the one who willingly
died the death of a slave out of love for them.

So look at him looking at you. And notice the love in his look.
Notice the humility. One of Saint Teresa's Sisters, who practiced
this method of prayer faithfully for hours on end, said she always
experienced dryness in prayer. When she was asked what she did
in prayer, she replied, *"I just allow myself to be loved!"*

Exercise 38:   The Heart of Christ

Here is yet another exercise for exposing yourself to the love of
Christ for you. I learned this one from an evangelical pastor who
seemed to have the gift for mediating the experience of Jesus
Christ, the Risen Lord, to people who asked to come in touch
with Christ. His method was something like this:

Let us suppose someone came to him and said, "I want to come
in touch with the Risen Lord." The pastor would lead him to a

quiet corner. They would both close their eyes and bow their heads in prayer.

The pastor would then say something like this to the other person: "Listen carefully to what I have to say now: Jesus Christ, the Risen Lord, is present here and now with us. Do you believe this?" After a pause the man would say, "Yes, I believe it."

"Now I am going to get you to consider something that is even more difficult to believe. Jesus Christ, the Risen Lord who is present here, loves and accepts you just as you are . . . You do not have to change to get his love . . . You do not have to become better, to get out of your sinful ways . . . He obviously wants you to become better, he obviously wants you to give up your sin, but you do not have to do this to get his love and his acceptance. *That* you have already, right now, just as you are, even before you decide to change, and whether you decide to change or not . . . Do you believe this? . . . Take your time over it . . . Then decide whether you believe it or not."

After some reflection the man would say, "Yes, I believe that, too."

"Well, then," says the pastor, "say something to Jesus. Say it aloud."

The man begins to pray aloud to the Lord . . . and it isn't long before he grasps the pastor's hand and says, "I know exactly what you mean when you speak about experiencing him. He is here! I can sense his presence!"

Sheer imagination? A special charisma given to our good pastor? Perhaps. The fact is that, whether or not this method is adequate for putting a person in contact with the Risen Lord, the doctrine on which it is based is certainly a sound one and the method certainly conducive to making a person feel the infinite treasures of the love of Christ. Try it for yourself:

Recall the presence of the Risen Lord . . . Tell him you believe he is present here with you . . .

Reflect on the fact that he loves and accepts you just as you are now . . . Take time out to sense his unconditional love for you as he looks at you *lovingly and humbly*.

Speak to Christ . . . or just stay lovingly in silence and communicate with him beyond words.

The devotion to the heart of Christ, so vigorous some years ago, so much on the decline today, would flourish once again if people would understand that it consists essentially in accepting Jesus Christ as love incarnate, as the manifestation of the unconditional love of God for us. Anyone who accepts this is bound to experience fruits *beyond all his expectations* in his own prayer life and in his apostolate. The great turning point in your life comes not when you realize that you love God but when you realize and fully accept the fact that God loves you unconditionally.

It is customary at retreats for retreatants to ask themselves those three questions made famous by the *Spiritual Exercises* of Saint Ignatius: *"What have I done for Christ? What am I doing for Christ? What am I going to do for Christ?"* The answer to the third question generally takes the form of all sorts of generous actions and sacrifices that the retreatant desires to perform as an expression of his love for Christ. My suggestion to retreatants is this: There is nothing you can do for Christ that will give him greater pleasure than that you believe in his love, his unconditional love for you. You will probably find that doing that is more difficult than some of the generous sacrifices you were planning to make and that it brings infinitely greater spiritual joy and spiritual progress than all the things you could *do* for Christ. After all, is there anything that you desire more from someone you love deeply than that he believe in your love and accept it fully?

Exercise 39: The Name as Presence

The practice of the Jesus Prayer has sometimes led people into giving the name of Jesus a value that is almost superstitious, leading even to adoration of the name. The name of Jesus is no more than a means for leading us to Jesus himself, and the loving recitation of his name, if it does not bring us into his presence, is worthless.

After quietening yourself, pronounce the name of Jesus slowly . . . Feel the presence of Jesus grow on you . . .

In what form do you experience his presence? As light . . . ? As devotion and unction . . . ? As darkness and dryness . . . ?

When the Presence becomes vivid, rest in it . . . When the Presence tends to dim, take up the recitation of his name again . . .

Exercise 40:   The Prayer of Intercession

We know very little about Jesus's way of praying. That will always be the closely guarded secret of those mountaintops and desert places to which he retired when he wanted to spend time in prayer.

We know his familiarity with the psalms, which he must have recited like every devout Jew. And we know of his practice of interceding for those he loved: *"Simon, Simon! Listen! Satan has received permission to test all of you, as a farmer separates the wheat from the chaff. But I have prayed for you, Simon, that your faith will not fail."* Here is one brief indication, in Luke's gospel (22:31), of what Jesus did in his time of prayer. He practiced the prayer of intercession.

We have another indication in John's gospel (17:9 ff.): *"I pray for them. I do not pray for the world but for the men you gave me . . . O holy Father, keep them safe by the power of the name you gave me, so they may be one just as you and I are one . . . I do not pray only for them but also for those who believe in me because of their message. I pray that they may all be one . . . O Father, may they be one in us, just as you are in me and I am in you. May they be one, so that the world will believe that you sent me."* Intercession again!

Scripture also tells us that this is the function of Jesus Christ today. His office of Redeemer is over. He has now taken on the office of Intercessor: *"Jesus lives on for ever, and his work as priest does not pass on to someone else. And so he is able, now and always, to save those who come to God through him, because he lives for ever to plead with God for them"* (Heb. 7:24–25). *"Who will accuse God's chosen people? God himself declares them not guilty! Can anyone, then, condemn them? Christ Jesus is the one who died or, rather, who was raised to life and is at the right side of God. He pleads with God for us"* (Rom. 8:33–34).

This is the form of prayer, together with petition, of which I shall speak presently, that Jesus recommended to his disciples. *"There is a great harvest, but few workers to gather it in. Pray to the owner of the harvest that he will send out more workers to gather in his harvest"* (Matt. 9:37–38). All sorts of objections come to mind: Why should we ask God for something he already knows we need? And it is his harvest, moreover. Doesn't he know it is in need of workers?

Jesus seems to brush aside all these objections and to announce a mysterious law of the world of prayer, namely, that God, by his own decree, has somehow placed his power in the hands of persons who intercede, in such a way that unless they intercede his power is withheld.

This is the great attraction of the prayer of intercession: that as you practice it you get a sense of the tremendous power there is in prayer. And having sensed this power you will never give up prayer. It is only at the end of this world that we shall realize how the destinies of persons and nations have been shaped, not so much by the external actions of powerful men and by events that seemed inevitable, but by the quiet, silent, irresistible prayer of persons the world will never know.

Father Teilhard de Chardin speaks in his book *The Divine Milieu* of a nun praying in a chapel in a desert place and, as she prays, all the forces of the universe seem to reorganize themselves in keep-

ing with the desires of that tiny praying figure and the axis of the
world seems to pass through that desert chapel. And James says,
*"The prayer of a righteous man has a powerful effect. Elijah was the same
kind of person that we are. He prayed earnestly that there would be no rain,
and no rain fell on the land for three and a half years. Once again he
prayed, and the sky poured out its rain and the earth produced its crops"*
(James 5:16–18).

It is enough to glance through the letters of Saint Paul to
realize how very much he made use of intercessory prayer in his
apostolate. He was not much of a speaker, as he himself concedes
to the Corinthians. But he was mighty in the performing of mira-
cles. And he was mighty in prayer. Here is a sample of how he
would intercede for his people: *"For this reason, then, I fall on my
knees before the Father, from whom every family in heaven and on earth
receives its true name. I ask God, from the wealth of his glory, to give you
power through his Spirit to be strong in your inner selves, and that Christ
will make his home in your hearts, through faith. I pray that you may have
your roots and foundations in love, and that you, together with all God's
people, may have the power to understand how broad and long and high and
deep is Christ's love. Yes, may you come to know his love—although it can
never be fully known—and so be completely filled with the perfect fullness of
God. To him who is able to do so much more than we can ever ask for, or
even think of, by means of the power working in us: to God be the glory in the
church and in Christ Jesus, for all time, for ever and ever! Amen"* (Eph.
3:14–21).

*"I thank my God for you all every time I think of you; and every time I
pray for you, I pray with joy . . . This is my prayer for you: I pray that
your love will keep on growing more and more, together with true knowledge
and perfect judgment, so that you will be able to choose what is best"* (Phil.
1:3–4, 9–10).

There is barely a letter of his in which he does not assure his
Christians that he is praying for them constantly, or asking for
their prayers for himself: *"For this reason, keep alert and never give up;
pray always for all God's people. And pray also for me, that God will give
me a message, when I am ready to speak, that I may speak boldly and make*

known the gospel's secret. For the sake of this gospel I am an ambassador,
though now I am in prison. Pray, therefore, that I may be bold in speaking
of it, as I should" (Eph. 6:18–20).

You may be one of those persons whom the Lord calls, in a very
special way, to exercise the ministry of intercession and to transform the world and the hearts of men by the power of their
prayers. *"Nothing is so powerful on earth as purity and prayer,"* says
Father Teilhard. If you have received this call from God, then
intercession will be your most common form of prayer. Even if
you have not received the call to exercise the ministry of intercession in a special way, you will frequently feel impelled by God to
intercede on various occasions. There are many ways of practicing this form of prayer. Here is one:

Spend some time in becoming aware of the presence of Jesus
and in getting in touch with him . . .

Imagine that Jesus floods you with his life and light and
power . . . See the whole of your being, in imagination, lit up
by this light that comes from him . . .

Now conjure up in imagination, one by one, the persons you
wish to pray for. Lay your hands on each person, communicating to him or her all the life and power that you have just
received from Christ . . . Take your time over each individual
. . . Call down Christ's love on him wordlessly . . . See him
light up with Christ's life and love . . . See him transformed . . .

Then move on to the next person . . . and the next . . .

It is extremely important that you become aware of Jesus and
get in touch with him at the beginning of your intercessory
prayer. Otherwise your intercession is in danger of becoming not
prayer, but a mere exercise of remembering people. The danger
is that your attention will be focused only on the people you are
praying for and not on God.

After you have prayed for some people in the form suggested
in the exercise, it is helpful to rest a while again in Christ's

presence, drinking in his power, his Spirit, and then continue your intercession, laying hands on yet other persons.

After praying in this way for each of the persons you love, pray for those who are committed to your care. Pastors should pray for their flocks . . . parents for their children . . . teachers for their pupils . . .

Then, after another pause to take in Christ's love and power, begin to pray for your "enemies," for Jesus has made it an obligation for us to pray for them. Lay your hands in blessing on each one of the persons whom you dislike . . . or who dislike you . . . on those who have caused you any kind of hurt . . . Feel Christ's power pass through your hands to their hearts . . .

Then move on to praying for whole nations . . . for the Church . . . The treasures of Christ are infinite and you need not fear that you will exhaust them by lavishing them on whole nations and peoples . . .

Leave your mind blank for a while, and allow the Spirit to suggest persons and causes to pray for . . . As some person comes to your mind, lay your hands on him, in the name of Christ . . .

It has been my experience as retreat director that some persons, when they attain a deep sense of union with God, feel impelled by him to intercede for others. They are initially worried that this may be a distraction, until they discover that they were brought to this state of deep union with God precisely so that they might intercede for their fellow men and that this intercession, far from distracting them, actually leads them deeper into union with God.

If you have been called to the ministry of intercession, there is something else you will discover from the frequent practice of intercessory prayer—that the more you lavish Christ's treasures on others, the more he floods your own heart and life with them. So that in praying for others, you yourself become enriched.

Exercise 41: Petition

Petition was almost the only form of prayer that Jesus taught his disciples when they asked him to teach them to pray. One can hardly claim to have been taught to pray by Christ himself if one has not learned the practice of petitionary prayer.

We are told in Luke 11: *"One time Jesus was praying in a certain place. When he finished, one of his disciples said to him, 'Lord, teach us to pray, just as John taught his disciples.' Jesus said to them, 'This is what you should pray: Father, may your name be kept holy. May your kingdom come. Give us day by day the food we need. Forgive us our sins, for we forgive everyone who has done us wrong. And do not bring us to hard testing.'"*

Every one of those phrases in the Lord's Prayer is a petition! Now listen to the commentary that the Lord himself gives to this prayer. This will be part of the exercise:

And Jesus said to his disciples: *"Suppose one of you should go to a friend's house at midnight and tell him, 'Friend, let me borrow three loaves of bread. A friend of mine who is on a trip has just come to my house and I don't have a thing to offer him!' And suppose your friend should answer from inside, 'Don't bother me! The door is already locked, my children and I are in bed, and I can't get up to give you anything.' Well, what then? I tell you, even if he will not get up and give you the bread because he is your friend, yet he will get up and give you everything you need because you are not ashamed to keep on asking.*

"And so I say to you: Ask, and you will receive; seek, and you will find; knock, and the door will be opened to you. For everyone who asks will receive, and he who seeks will find, and the door will be opened to him who knocks. Would any one of you fathers give his son a snake when he asks for a fish? Or would you give him a scorpion when he asks for an egg? As bad as you are, you know how to give good things to your children. How much more, then, the Father in heaven will give the Holy Spirit to those who ask him!" (Luke 11:1–13).

The words are startling in their simplicity: "Ask, and you will receive . . . For *everyone* who asks will receive . . ."

Imagine you hear Jesus saying those words to you. Ask yourself, "Do I really believe these words? What sense do they make to me?"

Then share your answers to these questions with Jesus.

You may do the same with Luke 18:1–6.

Or take these passages: *On his way back to the city the next morning, Jesus was hungry. He saw a fig tree by the side of the road and went to it, but found nothing on it except leaves. So he said to the tree, "You will never again bear fruit!" At once the fig tree dried up. The disciples saw this and were astounded. "How did the fig tree dry up so quickly?" they asked. "Remember this!" Jesus answered. "If you believe, and do not doubt, you will be able to do what I have done to this fig tree; not only this, you will even be able to say to this hill, 'Get up and throw yourself in the sea,' and it will. If you believe, you will receive whatever you ask for in prayer"* (Matt. 21:18–22).

Early next morning, as they walked along the road, they saw the fig tree. It was dead all the way down to the roots. Peter remembered what had happened and said to Jesus, "Look, Teacher, the fig tree you cursed has died!" Jesus said to them: "Remember this! If you have faith in God, you can say to this hill, 'Get up and throw yourself in the sea.' If you do not doubt in your heart but believe that what you say will happen, it will be done for you. For this reason I tell you: When you pray and ask for something, believe that you have received it and everything will be given you. And when you stand praying, forgive whatever you have against anyone, so that your Father in heaven will forgive your sins. If you do not forgive others, neither will your Father in heaven forgive your sins" (Mark 11:20–26).

After you have dwelt on one or other of these passages and spoken to Jesus about them, quieten yourself in preparation for petitionary prayer . . .

Forgive each person against whom you have a grievance . . . Say to each one in imagination, "I forgive you with all my heart in the name of Jesus Christ, just as the Lord has forgiven me . . ."

Now ask the Lord to fill your heart with the faith that makes petitionary prayer omnipotent . . . "Lord, I believe, help my unbelief . . ."

Now ask for the gift you want from the Lord: health, success in some enterprise . . .

Imagine the Lord giving this gift to you and imagine yourself joyfully praising him for this . . . Imagine the Lord withholding the gift from you and at the same time flooding your heart with peace and yourself joyfully praising him for this . . .

Exercise 42:   Jesus the Saviour

This is another form of practicing the Jesus Prayer. The recitation of the name of Jesus not only brings the presence of Jesus with it but also brings the salvation of Jesus to the one who is praying. Jesus is essentially the Saviour. That is what his name means (Matt. 1:21). *"Salvation is to be found through him alone; for there is no one else in all the world whose name God has given to men by whom we can be saved"* (Acts 4:12).

The loving recitation of the name of Jesus makes Jesus present to us. When Jesus becomes present he gives us his salvation. What kind of salvation? The salvation he brought in Palestine two thousand years ago: Healing for all our illnesses, physical, emotional, and spiritual, and, as a result, peace with our fellow men and with God and with ourselves.

I have already spoken before about the healing properties of the devout recitation of God's name. Mahatma Gandhi would speak of his form of prayer as "the poor man's medicine." The name of Jesus heals us of every one of our illnesses if we recite his name over each one of our wounds and illnesses with faith.

The recitation of Jesus's name also brings us the forgiveness of all our sins. There is a story in India of a king who had murdered

his brothers and then, in a mood of repentance, went to a saintly
hermit in search of penance and forgiveness. The hermit was
away when the king arrived. One of the hermit's disciples took it
upon himself to give the king his penance. He said, "Recite the
name of God three times and all your sins will be forgiven."
When the hermit returned and found out what his disciple had
done he was indignant. He said to his disciple, "Don't you know
that if you lovingly pronounce the name of God just once it is
enough to wash away the sins of a whole kingdom? Then how did
you dare tell the king to recite God's name three times? Are you
so totally lacking in faith in the power of God's name?"

Recite the name of Jesus slowly and lovingly, pausing every
now and then . . . desiring to be filled with the presence of
Jesus . . .

Now "anoint" each of your senses and faculties with the
name of Jesus. Scripture says, *"Your name is ointment poured out."*
(Song of Songs 1:3). So apply the ointment of this name to
your eyes, your feet, your heart . . . your memory, your understanding, your will, your imagination . . . As you do this,
see each sense, each limb, each faculty light up with the presence and power of Jesus, till your whole body, your whole
being, is alight and aglow with his presence.

Now go on to anoint other people with this name . . . Recite it with faith and love over each one of them . . . over the
sick and ailing . . . over your friends . . . over troubled people and the persons who are in the healing ministry, doctors,
nurses, counselors, pastors . . . over those you love . . . See
each one of them strengthened and made fully alive by his
powerful name . . .

Each time you become tired, return to the presence of Jesus
and rest there for a while . . .

Exercise 43:   Gospel Sentences

For this exercise you will have to make a list of some of the orders and questions that Jesus addressed to others in the gospels. Statements like, *"Come, follow me . . . Come and see . . . Feed my lambs . . . Launch out into the deep . . . I shall make you fishers of men . . . Watch and pray . . ."* Questions like, *"Who do you say that I am? . . . Do you love me? . . . Do you believe that I can do this? . . . What do you want me to do for you? . . . Do you want to be cured? . . ."*

Choose one of the questions or invitations from this list and begin the exercise:

Imagine you see the Risen Lord before you . . . Then imagine you hear him address to you one of these questions or invitations: *"Come and see . . . Do you love me? . . ."*

Do not reply immediately to his call or to his question . . . Imagine you hear him repeat his words again and again . . . Let those words resound in your whole being . . .

Keep listening to those words . . . let them challenge you, wake you, provoke you to a response . . . until you can hold back your response no longer. Then say to the Lord what your heart dictates.

A devout and frequent reading of the Scriptures, chiefly of the New Testament, brings a great richness to your prayer, and to your life. You will gradually discover those passages and phrases through which the Lord seems to communicate with you in a special way.

And frequently in time of distress and need, or joy, or solitude the Lord will say those words again to you in your heart and, through them, establish contact with you. And your heart will burn as did the hearts of the disciples at Emmaus when they heard the Lord explain to them the words of the Scriptures.

Exercise 44:   Holy Desires

This is a simple and delightful form of prayer inspired by a phrase used frequently by Ignatius of Loyola: *"Prayers and holy desires."* He tells young Jesuits who are studying for the priesthood that they must give all their time to their studies, as a result of which they will not have much time for prayer. But they can make up for this loss in time of prayer by their *holy desires* to do great things for God and for the good of their neighbors. He tells the Superiors of his communities that their first duty as Superiors is to *carry their communities on their shoulders* through their prayers (intercessory prayer for the members of their communities) and holy desires (desiring great things for their communities).

Ignatius himself was a man of great and intense desires, which is what made him the outstanding saint he is. At the time of his conversion he indulged in an exercise that can best be termed *holy daydreaming,* by means of which he fostered his desire to do great things for God. He would see himself in fantasy undertaking great and difficult enterprises for God. He would recall the great exploits of the saints and say to himself, *"Saint Francis did such and such for the Lord. I shall do more. Saint Dominic did these great deeds for the Lord. I shall do more . . . ."* He tells us that this holy exercise always left him with a feeling of peace and devotion and strength that he later termed spiritual consolation.

Saint Teresa of Ávila too would insist a great deal on the explicit fostering of great desires. She urges this chiefly on beginners: Let them begin with a sense of joy and freedom, she says, with great courage, full of desire to excel in God's service, for His Majesty loves courageous and daring souls.

This makes good psychological sense. You can hardly achieve what you cannot even *see* in imagination. You must be a man of great desires and of a great vision if you are going to be mighty in achievement.

There are two parts to this exercise. The first deals with holy desires for others, the second with holy desires for yourself:

Place before God the desires you have for each one of the people you wish to pray for . . . See each one of them, in imagination, as having the things you desire for them . . . You need not make an explicit prayer for them. It is enough to expose God to your holy desires . . . and to see those desires fulfilled.

What you have done for individuals, do now for families and groups and communities . . . for nations, for the Church . . . Have the courage to overcome all defeatism and pessimism and desire and hope for great things . . . and see these great things as actually fulfilled by the mighty power of God . . .

Now place before God the desires you have for yourself: Expose him to all the great things you desire to do in his service . . . The fact that you will never actually do them, or that you feel incapable of doing them, is irrelevant . . . What is important is that you gladden the heart of God by showing him how immense your desires are even though your strength is very small . . . it is thus that lovers speak when they express the immensity of their desires, which far outdistance their limited capacity . . .

There is another way of doing this. Imagine the great deeds of some of the saints: Saint Paul, Saint Francis Xavier . . . or any other saint you love and admire . . . Make those great deeds your own through desiring them, willing them, even performing them in fantasy . . . Identify with the saints in their great love . . . Fantasize that you yourself, by God's grace, are doing all that they did, suffering all that they suffered out of love for him . . . and give vent in fantasy to the ardent desires which your weakness will not allow you to fulfill in reality . . .

Then express to God the desires you have for the day that

lies ahead of you . . . all that you desire to do in his service
. . . See yourself, in imagination, actually being what you desire to be and acting as you desire to act . . .

In a world in which we give so much importance to achievement, we are apt to overlook the tremendous value of desires,
especially when achievements do not immediately follow on
them.

Exercise 45:   God-centeredness

When Jesus was asked by his disciples to teach them to pray, he
taught them to say, *"Father in heaven, hallowed be your name, your
kingdom come, your will be done . . ."* He begins with his Father, with
his Father's kingdom, his Father's interests. We are accustomed
to think of Jesus as being the man for others, and so, indeed, he
was. But we are apt to overlook the fact that he was primarily the
man for his Father. He was essentially a God-centered man.

We today are in danger of becoming overly man-centered. We
are unfamiliar with the sentiments of the psalmist, who looks up
to the mountains from where his help is to come. We are in
danger of being too earthbound and of overlooking the transcen-
dent in our lives, without which man ceases to be fully man.

This exercise is meant as a help toward making our lives more
God-centered.

Make a list of as many of your desires as you can remember
. . . the great desires, the small ones, the "romantic" desires,
the prosaic ones . . .
Make a list of some of the problems you are grappling with
. . . family problems, job problems, personality problems . . .
Now ask yourself: What part am I giving to God in the fulfillment of these desires of mine?

Does he play a role in making these desires come true? What role? Am I satisfied with the role he has? Is he?

Then ask yourself: What part am I giving to God in the solution of the problems that I am dealing with currently? . . . How much am I relying on him in solving them? . . . How much trust do I have in him? . . .

Yet another question: Where does God feature in my list of desires? . . . Is he one of the things I desire? . . . How much? . . .

Where does the search for God feature in my list of problems? . . .

Now take one desire or one problem at a time. Ask yourself: How do I attempt to fulfill this desire? How do I generally attempt to solve this problem? Work this out in fantasy . . . See yourself going about meeting your desires and solving your problems . . . Notice all the means you employ to do this . . .

Now expose every one of these *means* to God and to his influence . . . What is important here is *exposure,* not results . . . See every action, thought, etc., as coming from God and moving toward God . . . Notice how you feel as you do this . . .

Exercise 46:   Living Flame of Love

I got the inspiration for this exercise from that admirable book *The Cloud of Unknowing,* which speaks so charmingly of a blind stirring of love that arises within our hearts and goes out toward God.

Spend some time quieteting yourself through one of the awareness exercises . . .

Imagine now that you go down to the very depths of your being, or the center of your being. All is darkness . . . but you find there a fountain that bubbles up toward God. Or imagine that you find there a living flame of love shooting up toward God . . .

I want you to put a word or a very brief phrase to the rhythm of that flame or that fountain . . . just the name of Jesus . . . or Abba . . . or Come, Holy Spirit . . . or my God and my All . . .

Listen to that word being uttered in the depths of your being . . . Do not pronounce it. You hear it faintly, as coming from far, far away . . . from the very depths of your being . . .

Now imagine that the sound grows and begins gradually to fill your whole being, so that you hear it in your head, your chest, your stomach . . . the whole of your body . . .

After a while imagine you hear it fill the whole room . . . then, all the surroundings . . . Then it grows in intensity and fills all the earth, and the heavens . . . so that the whole universe resounds with this word that emanates from the depths of your heart . . .

Rest in that word . . . and now, if you wish, pronounce it lovingly yourself . . .

Exercise 47: The Prayer of Praise

If I had to choose the one form of prayer that has made the presence of Christ most real in my life and given me the deepest sense of being supported and surrounded by the loving providence of God, I would unhesitatingly choose this, the last form of prayer I propose in this book, the Prayer of Praise. I would also choose it for the great peace and joy it has so often brought me in times of distress.

The prayer consists, quite simply, of praising and thanking God for everything. It is based on the belief that nothing happens in our lives that is not foreseen and planned by God—just nothing, not even our sins.

God obviously does not want sin. He obviously did not want that greatest of all sins, the murder of Jesus Christ. And yet Scripture quite shockingly tells us again and again that the passion and death of Christ *was written* and had to be gone through. Saint Peter confirms this in his sermon to the Jews (Acts 2:23): *"God, in his own will and knowledge, had already decided that Jesus would be handed over to you; and you killed him . . ."* So Christ's murder was foreseen and planned.

Sin is obviously something that we must hate and avoid. Yet we can praise God even for our sins when we have repented, because he will draw great good from them. And so the Church, in an ecstasy of love, will sing at the Easter liturgy, *"O happy fault . . . O necessary sin of Adam!"* And Saint Paul explicitly tells the Romans, *"Where sin increased, God's grace increased much more . . . What shall we say, then? That we should continue to live in sin so that God's grace will increase? Certainly not!"* (Rom. 5:20; 6:1).

This is something we hardly dare think of: to thank and praise God even for our sins! It is right that we regret our sins. But, having done this, we must also learn to praise God for them. If Herod and Pilate had been converted, they would surely have repented the role they played in the Passion. They could then have praised him for having brought about the death and resurrection of Christ through the role they played in the Passion.

I have known so many people who go through life carrying a weight of guilt in their hearts for sins they have committed. One of them told me he experienced deep guilt, not over his sins, because he was sure they were forgiven, but over arriving a few minutes late at his father's deathbed. He simply couldn't shake off the guilt, no matter how hard he tried. What an immense relief and peace he felt when I got him to explicitly thank and praise God for having arrived late at his father's deathbed! Suddenly he sensed that all was well, all was in God's hands, God had some use even for this and would draw good even from this . . .

Try this yourself now:

Think of something in the past or present that is causing you pain or distress or guilt or frustration . . .

If you are in any way to blame for this thing, express your regret and sorrow to the Lord . . .

Now explicitly thank God for this, praise him for it . . . Tell him that you believe that even this fits into his plan for you and so he will draw great good from this for you and for others, even though you may not see the good . . .

Leave this thing and all the other events of your life, past, present, and to come, in the hands of God . . . and rest in the peace and relief that this will bring.

This is so much in keeping with Saint Paul's teaching to his Christians: *"Be joyful always, pray at all times, be thankful in all circumstances. This is what God wants of you in your life in Christ Jesus"* (1 Thess. 5:16–18). *"Speak to one another in the words of psalms, hymns, and sacred songs; sing hymns and psalms to the Lord, with praise in your heart. Always give thanks for everything to God the Father, in the name of our Lord Jesus Christ"* (Eph. 5:19–20). *"May you always be joyful in your life in the Lord. I say it again, rejoice! . . . Don't worry about anything, but in all your prayers ask God for what you need, always asking him with a thankful heart. And God's peace, which is far beyond human understanding, will keep your hearts and minds safe, in Christ Jesus"* (Phil. 4:4; 6–7).

Some people fear that praising God for everything may lead to a certain sluggishness and fatalism. This difficulty is more theoretical than practical. Anyone who has sincerely practiced this form of prayer knows that we make every possible effort on our part to do good and avoid evil and only then do we praise God for the outcome, whatever it may be.

The one danger I see in this form of prayer is not fatalism, but a repression of our unpleasant emotions. It is often necessary to grieve over losses that we suffer, or feel our anger and frustration, before we praise God and open our hearts to the joy and peace that this brings with it.

That peace and joy will become a fairly habitual disposition with us as we become accustomed to praise and thank God constantly. Where formerly we would have grown tense and worried over the many disappointments that life brings with it, even in minor situations (a train that comes late, bad weather when we are about to go outdoors, an unfortunate remark we inadvertently make in conversation . . .), we now set about calmly to do what we can on our part and cheerfully leave all the rest in God's hands, knowing that all shall be well, even though *at the moment* it doesn't seem to be so.

There is a Chinese story of an old farmer who had an old horse for tilling his fields. One day the horse escaped into the hills and when all the farmer's neighbors sympathized with the old man over his bad luck, the farmer replied, "Bad luck? Good luck? Who knows?" A week later the horse returned with a herd of wild horses from the hills and this time the neighbors congratulated the farmer on his good luck. His reply was, "Good luck? Bad luck? Who knows?" Then, when the farmer's son was attempting to tame one of the wild horses, he fell off its back and broke his leg. Everyone thought this very bad luck. Not the farmer, whose only reaction was, "Bad luck? Good luck? Who knows?" Some weeks later the army marched into the village and conscripted every able-bodied youth they found there. When they saw the farmer's son with his broken leg they let him off. Now was that good luck? Bad luck? Who knows?

Everything that seems on the surface to be an evil may be a good in disguise. And everything that seems good on the surface may really be an evil. So we are wise when we leave it to God to decide what is good luck and what bad, and thank him that all things turn out for good with those who love him. Then we will share something of that marvelous mystical vision of Dame Julian of Norwich, who uttered the loveliest and most consoling sentence I have ever read: *Sin is behovely, but all shall be well and all shall be well and all manner of thing shall be well."*